ISBN 0-87666-182-7

siamese cat book

The author, Mrs. Vera M. Nelson with three of her lovely Siamese. On the chair is Doneraile Dimple, an English import that had arrived by plane the day before this photo was taken, Petita of Ebon Mask is on the left, and Ch. Doneraile Drusilla, also an import and related to Dimple, is the last, but not least, of the trio.

SIAMESE CAT BOOK

by

VERA M. NELSON

Distributed in the U.S.A. by T.F.H. Publications, Inc., 211 West Sylvania Avenue, P.O. Box 27, Neptune City, N.J. 07753; in England by T.F.H. (Gt. Britain) Ltd., 13 Nutley Lane, Reigate, Surrey; in Canada to the book store and library trade by Clarke, Irwin & Company, Clarwin House, 791 St. Clair Avenue West, Toronto 10, Ontario; in Canada to the pet trade by Rolf C. Hagen Ltd., 3225 Sartelon Street, Montreal 382, Quebec; in Southeast Asia by Y.W. Ong, 9 Lorong 36 Geylang, Singapore 14; in Australia and the south Pacific by Pet Imports Pty. Ltd., P.O. Box 149, Brookvale 2100, N.S.W., Australia. Published by T.F.H. Publications, Inc. Ltd., The British Crown Colony of Hong Kong.

Photographs by: Ronald Marden, Sydney, George I. Davis, George Mayborn, Frank Bjerring, Curtis Mayborn, Ginia, Rimel Studio, E.D.R. Pruett, Lewis R. Berlepsch, Louise Van der Meid, Donald S. Herbert, Muzzie, Arthur Studio, Three Lions Inc., Frank J. Murray, Hulton Press Ltd., Sally Anne Thompson, Jeanne White, E. I. Blomstrann, Victor Baldwin, Sal Celeski, Marwayne Studios, and the author. Drawings by the author.

CONTENTS

Soft, cute, and lovable, a tiny bundle of vivacious affection and fluid mobility, yet with the wisdom of the ages reflected deep in its inquisitive eyes . . . this is the Siamese kitten.

FOREWORD

This book is dedicated to my husband, Sven, and my daughters, Charlotte and Penny, for without their patience and willingness to endure the inconvenience of having my time often taken up entirely by the Siamese, I could never have survived the vicissitudes of raising Siamese. In times of trouble, my family has stood by and helped me weather the storm, rejoiced with me in success, and sorrowed with me in failure.

The writer lays no claim to omniscience about Siamese, for there is always more to learn, and new experiences ahead. Knowledge of the Siamese is sometimes difficult for the novice to acquire, and it is the aim of this book to help the novice, and to provide something of interest even to the older breeder.

The information in this book is gathered entirely from my own years of breeding and showing Siamese, nursing them through illnesses, keeping them well, and winning and losing in competition at the shows. If it helps even a few younger breeders, it will have served its purpose, for to help others over some of the commoner pitfalls is my dearest wish.

Vera M. Nelson

Though the "sacred" Siamese Cat emerged from the exotic East where they inhabited the ancient temples of Siam and were labeled "sacred" by the priests, our modern specimens temper their archaic profundity with humor.

CHAPTER 1

ORIGIN
OF THE SIAMESE CAT

THE Siamese Cat is named for the land of its origin, that small country in the Orient which has so much of the exotic and interesting in its history and being. It seems only logical that an animal of such fascination as the Siamese should come from the East.

What steps were taken, genetically, to produce what we know as the Siamese Cat are not known, but the cats were first seen, according to legend, in the temples of Siam. They are sometimes referred to as the "Sacred Siamese," but there is no substantiated evidence that they were ever used in the religious rites of the temples, but rather, that they were kept as pets and "watch-cats" to warn the priests of intruders. The Siamese cats which were eventually exported from Siam were not obtained from the temples, but from families of royalty or wealth. It was considered a piece of great good fortune, by the commoners of Siam, to own a pair of Siamese cats, but the ownership by any but royalty was finally forbidden. According to rumor, the poorer people who came into possession of a pair of the cats sat back and waited for good luck to come their way, eventually falling into poverty and distress. Hence, ownership was limited to those who could afford such "fortune."

SIAMESE IN ENGLAND AND AMERICA

The first cats taken from Siam to England in the eighteen-eighties are the progenitors of most of the Siamese we know today. They were first seen in America in about 1903, when they made their appearance at a show, taking the fancy of the public, then, even as now. Today, in this country, more than half the yearly registrations of purebred cats are registrations of Siamese, so quickly has their popularity grown. The same proportion of Siamese to other breeds holds true in England, also.

It is never necessary to hunt for the Siamese section at a cat show. Just follow the crowd, and where it is thickest, that's where you'll find the Siamese. People usually either like them immediately or dislike them, but to some they are an acquired taste, like olives. They are so different from the average cat, either short or long-haired, that they seem to startle novices at first glimpse. To one of artistic inclination, they appeal immediately, for the beautiful contrast in color, the litheness of form, sleekness of coat, and clarity of outline make them attractive.

SIAMESE LEGENDS

Many stories are told to account for the peculiarities of the breed, the kinked tail and the squinted or crossed, eyes. My favorite is the one about the two cats who lived in a remote temple with an old priest. The elderly gentleman passed to his reward, and the cats were left without a guardian for the temple. Chula, the female, discussed the matter with her mate, Tien, and they decided that she should stay to watch over the one treasure of the temple, a jeweled cup, while Tien went in search of a young priest to take over the duties of the temple. Tien was gone for some weeks and poor Chula found her duties burdensome, so she solved the dilemma by curling her tail tightly about the stem of the cup, so that she could sleep, knowing that nobody could steal the chalice without waking her. During her waking hours, she stared fixedly at the cup, assuring herself that it was truly safe.

Tien returned, finally, with a young priest, and they found Chula still guarding the treasure faithfully, while her new kittens played about in the sunshine before her. They all had kinks in their tails and crossed eyes, due to prenatal influence. A rapid development of congenital deformity, I'd say! To this day, kinked tails are common, though considered a fault if noticeable, and crossed eyes are still seen occasionally.

The second tale of the kinked tail is rather cute, too. The Princess, bathing with her ladies in waiting one day, wanted to remove her rings and put them somewhere safe, so she slipped them over the cat's tail and tied a knot in the tail so that the rings could not slip off. The cat's descendants all had kinks in their tails.

COLOR VARIETIES

The Siamese is now recognized in four color variations in the United States. These are the Seal-Pointed, Chocolate-Pointed, Blue-Pointed and Frost-Pointed Siamese. The Seal-Point has a coat of

The mystery and the legends that surround the veiled and timeless past of the Siamese Cat are personified by this Egyptian bronze statue of great antiquity, a survivor from the past when the Land of the Nile was mighty and great Pharoahs built the pyramids and sphinx and the ancient tombs of kings.

pale fawn with the markings or "points"—mask, ears, legs and feet, and tail—of a deep seal-brown, almost black. The Blue-Point has a pale, cold body tone and the points are of a grayish-blue. The Chocolate-Point's coat is a pale ivory, unshaded, with points of deep milk-chocolate tone. The Frost-Point has an extremely pale, cold body color and points of a pale bluish-gray with a sort of blood-tone, or pinkish cast. All have blue eyes, varying in depth of color with depth of general pigmentation.

The Chocolate-Point and the Frost-Point have only in the past few years received championship status in America, though the Chocolate was recognized several years earlier in England. For some time the Chocolate-Pointed cats seen were like rather faded Seal-Points and not particularly attractive, but in recent years they have been improved tremendously and are certainly beautiful. The fundamental point of recognition in the Chocolate, which distinguishes him from the Seal, is the color of the nose pad and paws. This skin is a deep chocolate tone definitely brown in the Chocolate, while in the Seal it is black. Much the same difference tells which is Blue- and which is Frost-Pointed. The Blue-Point has nose leather and pads

Champion Lamar's Rocco, a Chocolate male son of Ch. Lamar's Toto. Breeder, Mrs. S. S. Dial; owner, Mrs. Charles Jones, Coronado, California.

The Seal-Point female, Champion Medicine Lake Texx-Ess Rose, bred and owned by Mrs. Adolph Olson, Minneapolis, Minnesota.

of a deep blue, while the Frost has leather of a bluish tone with a pinkish undercast and the paw pads of the Frost are pink, not blue.

Until recently there was no provision in the shows for exhibiting the Chocolate-Pointed Cats, and they were, if entered, shown as Seal-Points and, of course, penalized for lack of pigmentation. In most cases, the Chocolate-Points do not have as good type, structurally, as the Seals, being rather a throwback to the type the Seals of fifteen and twenty years ago carried. There are, of course, exceptions to this, and a few years will see the type immensely improved and the Chocolates as popular and lovely as the Blue- and Seal-Points are now.

Hybridizations have been done, using the Siamese in the experimental breedings, and some rather exotic and lovely cats have resulted from these hybrid breedings. The latest is the Red-Pointed cat, called by one breeder the "Flame Concha," a name which truly suits it. The coat is white with the points or markings a real red, though the mask is not as heavy nor well defined as that of the real Siamese. A long-haired Siamese, the cross having been made with both long-haired black and long-haired white cats, has been successfully bred, and is called the "Malayan Persian" or "Color Point". It

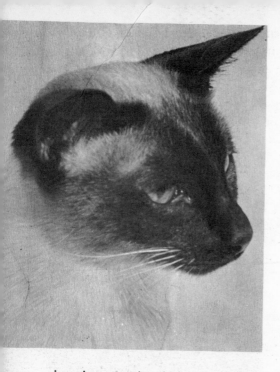

A beautiful head-study of Champion H.R.H. of Ebon Mask. Breeder-owners, Sven S. and Vera M. Nelson.

is quite attractive, but to the Siamese purist, the short, sleek coat is a part of the fascination of this breed and no variation can be as attractive.

The Red-Pointed cat is a cross between a self-red and a Seal-Pointed Siamese. If a self-red short-haired male is mated to a Seal-Point female, the resulting children will be, in variety of colors, black males and tortie females. The tortie females (in the genes) have restriction of "color to points" from their dam, and one of these tortie females, mated to a Seal-Point male, will produce, since she carries the genes for color restriction, red-pointed, tortie-pointed, black, tortie, and red kittens, as well as Seal-Points. All these color variations can appear, but one may have to mate the cats several times before the desired Red-Point will appear. Red-Point mated to Red-Point will produce Red-Points. But, I wonder how many genera-tions later a solid red or even a black cat may occur in a litter from Red-Points. We have seen Seal-Point breeding keep to its own color for several generations and then, a Blue-Point appears, the gene having been carried down for all those generations, finally combining through two cats to produce the recessive color. These Red-Pointed cats are an interesting experiment and may take the fancy of many lovers of cats, for they are attractive and odd.

Incidentally, it is interesting to note that many of the animals from Asia bear the contrasting pigmentation which is seldom seen in animals originating elsewhere. For example, there is the panda, black and white, with the color so very definitely divided into body, or basic, color and contrasting facial color; the Pekingese dog, which comes in many colors, the most popular of which is the fawn body with black mask; the Himalayan rabbit, white coated with small mask and ears, feet and tail of black; and finally, the Siamese cat with body and markings of such great contrast.

It has been hinted that the Blue-Pointed cat is the result of genetic changes resulting from matings between the Seal-Pointed Siamese Cat and a blue cat, called the Blue Cat of Korat. While the Siamese markings are recessive to all other feline colors, by mating hybrid offspring back to Siamese it is possible, following sure and set rules, to produce descendants which will carry characteristics of both original ancestors.

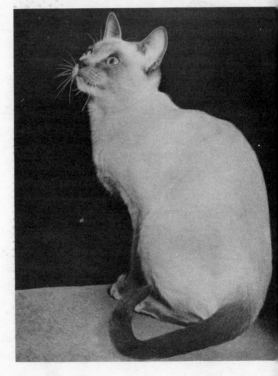

Grand Champion Vee Roi's Violet Lady, a lovely Blue-Point female, bred by Mrs. R. H. Hecht, and owned by Mrs. Alice Dugan, Hartsdale, New York.

Triple Champion Frost-Point Siamese, Ta-Lee-Ho's Frolik of Ramada, owned by Sol and Beatrice Gerlisky, California.

The Siamese has been used, also, in producing the "Burmese" cat, which, after some generations of scientific, genetically correct breeding, produces cats of a sable brown, with the points hardly distinguishable from the body color, and the eyes of a golden color. But the voice of the Siamese has remained true in these cats.

The Burmese cat has now been given recognition in this country by all five of the registering bodies. In the largest of these organizations, the Burmese may be entered in the Foundation Record upon sworn statement by the breeder that for four generations none but pure Burmese have resulted from the breedings. The fourth generation after the original registration in the Foundation Record will be eligible for Stud Book registration. The Burmese cat is, in type, very like the Siamese, but the color is of a sable brown with no appreciable difference seen between markings and basic body color, and the eyes are gold or yellow.

The Siamese Cat combines the grace of the panther, the fleetness of the deer, the softness of a downy chick, the strength of the lion, and the affection of the dog in one charming bundle.

Portrait head-study of a lovely Chocolate-Point Siamese
Cat owned by Mrs. Landers.

CHAPTER 2

CHARACTER OF THE SIAMESE CAT

THE character of the Siamese cat is one of definite lines, for he is a persistent, though ingratiating creature. What he wants, he wants now, not an hour from now, nor at your convenience, but NOW! Unless he gets it, he tells the world his tale of woe, or sulks like a spoiled child, whining about his troubles until you give in and grant his heart's desire.

The Siamese is affection personified on four feet, his demonstrations almost too much, at times. He loves you, and you must be so informed at very frequent intervals or he is unhappy. When you sit down, he sits, too—on you! This is very flattering, of course, but it can be disconcerting to have to spend some time removing what seems to be the major part of his coat from your clothing when he finally leaves you. You learn to dress for the cats—don't laugh, it's true! You find yourself, when you go shopping for a suit or dress, automatically thinking of how the cat hair will appear or be hidden.

When you go to bed, so does he, on top of the covers, or, if you are a soft-hearted soul, under them, pressed like a plaster to your back or side. This way you get a lullaby, of course, being sung to sleep to the tune of his thunderous purrs of satisfaction. It makes you feel that you must be a deserving creature to be honored with this demonstration of your worth.

Each Siamese has his or her own way of showing affection. My own dear pet sits in my lap and stares at my face, finally reaching up and patting me softly. Often I am roused during the night by her touch, and think she is assuring herself that I am really there with her. When I speak, she answers, and we carry on some very long and, I am sure, intelligent conversations. It does seem, after living with Siamese for many years, that one should understand them—their kittens do, and they are much younger than we. One does come to understand the hunger cry, which is a loud "mauwerr," and the meow of content, which is soft and well mixed with purrs.

Curiosity is perhaps the most notable characteristic of the Siamese.

Just open the refrigerator door and he'll appear, as if by magic, looking for a tidbit. One must be careful of doors, even those of refrigerators, for it is not rare for Baby to disappear, and the owner to search frantically for the lost lamb, only to remember that the last time she saw Baby was when she was at the "frig." A hurried yank at the door, and out comes Baby, rather crackly from the cold, his whiskers nicely frosted, and a look in his eye which expresses his satisfaction with the contents of the larder. He'll sleep for an hour or two in a warm spot and, by the grace of some feline guardian angel, be none the worse for his experience.

Linen closets, where all the nicely ironed sheets, cases, towels, and other things are kept, are full of fascination for Baby. At any opportunity he creeps in and enjoys his siesta among the linens. I'm afraid the neatness of the closet is not quite the same after his nap; but what matter, he's worth all the trouble he causes, and his tricks, though sometimes aggravating, are still amusing.

Quite naturally, advanced age (eight to twelve years) finds the energetic and active Siamese more rest-desiring. Thus, on days when our Petita, nearly thirteen now, feels kittenish, anything and everything into which she can hook her claws is tossed about, especially her toys. After such a "youthful" outburst, she will retire to a soft, cozy corner, or to my lap, for a needed rest. Instead of getting up mornings, she frequently remains curled in the blankets of my bed until the time my husband is due home. Petita is a lovely old cat, having a fine, heavy coat and attractive point color, but her eyes have faded.

Unquestionably, a serious drawback to raising cats is their short life-span—a fact we must face bravely. However, while they are in our company, they afford us a large measure of joy and happiness, even showing some understanding of human foibles and seemingly accepting us just as we are. All they ask is to be allowed to live with us and to share our lives as much as possible.

FEEDING THE SIAMESE

The Siamese is, on the average, a good eater, relishing his food, and eating what is put before him like the good trencherman he is. Sometimes, especially after an illness, he is apt to be a bit "picky" about his diet, but this soon passes, and after all, we humans are like that, too, so we should be able to understand and cater a little to his whims.

Should the kitten develop "whims" about food, such as a refusal to eat any but one chosen tidbit, he needs to be trained to eat what is put before him, not so much for the owner's convenience as for the kitten's own good. We feed all the kittens together from one large dish, for we have found that competition is the spice of appetite! I've been called by frantic new owners, after they have had the baby in their home for a couple of weeks, to be told that the kit won't eat anything but tuna, or kidney, or fish. My answer is always the same. Give him what you want him to eat, and what he needs, and if he has not finished it at the end of fifteen minutes remove the dish and do not offer him anything at all until his next big mealtime arrives. Offer him exactly the same food as he was offered before, and repeat the removal of the dish if he does not take the food. Surely you can

Champion Lamar's Toto, Chocolate-Point male, bred and owned by Lt. Commander and Mrs. Charles Jones, Coronado, California.

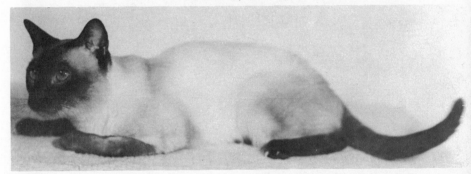

be as stubborn as he is, and I warn you that if you cannot, you are making a dictator who will rule you with an iron paw! I've found that when he is hungry enough he WILL eat what he is given, and once he finds that you will not cater to his notions he obliges by being a good chap and eating his meal quickly and completely.

FAVORITE AREAS

The Siamese loves warmth and comfort, and will soon ferret out the coziest spot in the house for his naps. In the cellar, beneath our dining-room, stands the big hot-water boiler, and one can almost always find a cat, or a pile of cats, tucked into the corner under the buffet, sleeping away the hours. The steel radiator cover in the living-room is another favored spot until it gets too hot, when we are asked, in no uncertain terms, to please put a magazine or paper on it to temper the heat. The cats lie there, letting their heads hang over the edge of the cover, in the blast of warm air rising from the radiator, paws and tail dangling over the edge, too, until one wonders that they don't just slide off to the floor. Small kittens cuddle under the radiators, but this I do not encourage, for it is apt to be too hot, and make them delicate. Sunny window sills are nearly always decorated by a Siamese stretched out full length absorbing the sunshine. The best woolen blanket or down puff automatically becomes "his."

The beautiful Blue-Point female, Grand Champion Vee Roi's Lantara Gene. Breeder-owner, Mrs. R. H. Hecht, Normandy, Missouri.

One's favorite chair is his top choice, too, and I often find myself perched on the very edge of my chair, watching television, while the cats pile in a heap behind me, taking up almost the whole seat. You say, "Well, why not put them down?" It's hardly worth the reproach-ful looks, so either I perch or find myself another, less favored chair. Those of you who are owned by a Siamese will understand, and those of you who will some day live with a Siamese will learn.

Unless you have patience, don't choose a Siamese for a pet. He's a problem child, and if you value your curtains and furnishings above the satisfaction of his companionship and beauty, he's not for you. He's as sweet as a sugar-plum one day, and the next he's a feral creature, stalking some prey, which, according to him, never is in the open, but is under each piece of furniture, or on top of it, inside every closet, and must, simply must be caught. Your Siamese is no "sit on a cushion, strawberries and cream" creature, no indeed. He's a bundle of activity, full of life and zest, interested in all you do, sharing everything with you, big-hearted, generous creature he is, and expecting you to do the same. He'll even try to share your bath, not to speak of your meals!

The Siamese is not sneaky, just clever. Whatever he wants, he will take right from under your nose. Though you may try to outwit him, he is likely to get the best of you nine times out of ten. For example, Dru, one of our cats, always managed to get with me into the pantry, which contains a washing machine, shelves for dishes, and storage for various foods. Invariably, Dru would hide under or behind the washing machine, where absent-mindedly I would leave her—to gorge herself until my other cats succeeded in calling my attention to this unfairness of allowing Dru into forbidden quarters, but shutting them out!

It takes patience to adjust to life with the Siamese, but one compensation is that one is never bored. Strangely enough, it is a fact that Siamese are very attractive to men, more so than any other breed of cat. It is understandable, in a way, for the Siamese has many doglike characteristics. He's a born retriever, fetching anything thrown for him and returning it to have it tossed again. He'll keep this up until you are exhausted—he never seems to be! The Siamese, if one starts when he is a young cat, will train easily to a lead and harness. I dislike collars because of the danger that the cat may catch the collar on some projection and hang himself up on it, but there are collars made of elastic which will stretch and slip over the head. Some breeders dislike the harness because they say it may throw out the bones of the shoulders, but I have never had any difficulty with this. It seems the safer of the two choices.

One must learn to understand the Siamese in order to cope with his ways. He is much like a small child in his reactions to upsetting events and times. Jealousy is rampant in the Siamese and his resentment of any encroachment upon what he considers his possessions or rights may be demonstrated by naughtiness or spitefulness. I have known kittens or cats who have come "unhousebroken" for no reason that their owners could see, but close questioning revealed that some major change had taken place in the household within recent weeks. My advice has been that the owners be firm about this, that they provide every possible opportunity for the cat to have a sanitary pan within easy access and then, if he persists in his misbehavior, that he be penned up each time the accident occurs—if it can be called an accident! When the happening is due to spite or pique, the cat will usually pick one rug or one spot, such as a particular scatter mat or some soft article or piece of furniture. I advise putting him in the bathroom or in a cage for twenty-four hours, after he has been coldly and severely scolded in a firm and somewhat louder voice than usual. He is not stupid, you know, and soon gets the idea of the reason for this terrible attitude upon the part of his beloved! Be as persistent as he is, and put him in limbo each time he misbehaves, for a period of from six to twenty-four hours. He'll soon act again as he should.

THE SIAMESE VOICE

One drawback, if it can be called that, of the Siamese is his voice. He is not a cat for a small apartment, or for close quarters. The Siamese has a much heavier voice than the domestic or the Persian cat, deeper in tone and much louder. The grown male has a "meowrrr" that carries for an unbelievable distance, and the female, while her ordinary voice is simply loud, screams so when in season, or heat, that she is a most undesirable neighbor for those who do not, like

Champion Newton's Tayoh and his dam, Grand Champion Newton's Desiree, bred and owned by Mrs. A. C. Cobb, of Newton, Massachusetts.

ourselves, adore these cats. The calling of a Siamese female has to be heard to be believed. It does not seem possible that one small cat can make such a commotion.

So, I offer this advice. If you intend your Siamese to be just a pet, have him, or her, neutered, and it will do away with much of the nuisance of the loud voice, for the neutered cat is not so persistently talkative as a natural male or female. Too, an unaltered male does not make a good house pet. That old biological urge causes him to spray, and believe me, one does not wish to live in an atmosphere of "tom-cat." It used to be considered quite an ordeal for an animal to go through the operation for castration or spaying, but surgery has progressed for the animals, as for humans, to the point where danger is negligible. We have had females spayed at five and six years of age, cats that were breeding queens, and have had female kittens spayed at three months, and (with crossed fingers I say this) have not yet lost a female due to the operation. You will be much happier, and so will the cat, if the neutering is done at an early age so that the kitten never develops any urge to have contact with the opposite sex.

TRAVELING SIAMESE

Many Siamese train well to travel by car, and a number of owners of kittens from here have come to call, their cats riding comfortably in the automobile with them. Your Siamese likes to be where you are and do what you do, so train him early, and you'll never be lonely for he'll be a faithful companion all his life. There is no easier way to make acquaintances than to have your Siamese in your car with you. People just can't seem to get over the sight of a cat acting like a dog, and the Siamese is a source of interest and attention to practically everyone. Naturally!

Siamese kittens at five weeks of age. Soft and cuddly
they have all the charm for which this species of feline
is deservedly noted.

CHAPTER 3

BUYING A SIAMESE KITTEN

L ET us suppose that you, a novice, have seen a picture of a
Siamese cat, and that you, like so many, have been fascinated
by the strangeness and beauty of the cat. A time arrives when you
want to get a pet, and you recall the Siamese and decide that you'd
like to have one of "those cats." The problem now is to find a Siamese! Though they are so popular they are still not common, and many
people have never seen a Siamese. In the Sunday papers of any good-
sized city there are columns of pet ads, and in these you will sometimes see advertisements of Siamese kits for sale. There are, too, the
magazines, both those catering only to the Cat Fancy, and those
which have sections devoted to different kinds of pets, including
cats. There is the **Cats Magazine** in which breeders from all parts
of the country advertise their stock. This magazine prints show reports
and information about the winners in all the large cat shows in the
United States.

If you are looking for a pet kitten, conformation to the judging
standard is not of real importance, unless you are one of those who
cannot enjoy a possession unless it is the best obtainable. Disposition
is of great importance in either pet or breeding cat.

The better the cat, the handsomer he'll be, so it will be to your
own interest to look the field over, seeing as many Siamese as possible
before buying.

To one who is anticipating breeding the kitten when it reaches
maturity, quality is of the essence. Pedigree is important, too, in
order that one may do judicious breeding, not just to swell the number of Siamese, but to produce the "better" Siamese.

BREEDERS AND PET SHOPS

Breeders, when a prospective buyer visits, will gladly explain the
pedigrees of the cats and show the good points of the animals. Here
we must explain that pedigrees which show direct importations from
England will seldom show as many champions in the four genera-

tions of background as will pedigrees of American-bred cats. English championships are won hard, the cat having to win three shows under three different judges to qualify for a full championship. In the United States a cat could win, until recently, all his championship points under one judge, who might officiate at several shows in one season. Too, we have more championship shows in America than in England, where many shows are really exhibitions, not certified to award championship certificates.

Pet kittens usually sell for reasonable prices, and quite a number of breeders will have the kittens altered and given their inoculations for infectious enteritis before sale. This does add to the price, but saves the new owner from the worry of having to do all these things for the kitten.

Kittens bought for breeding stock are usually sold at about four months of age and have had their inoculations to protect them as far as possible against illness. The prices for breeding stock vary according to the excellence of the individual specimen, and one must rely to a great extent upon the judgment of the breeder in picking a kitten from a litter. Breeders and pet shops are anxious to give good value for the price asked, for their reputations depend upon the performance of the stock they sell, as well as upon that of their own breeding stock. Prices range from $15 for poor specimens for pets to $200 for good breeding stock. The buyer pays not only for the kitten, but for its pedigree. In cats, as in everything else, you get what you pay for, there are no bargains except in very exceptional cases.

REGISTRATION ORGANIZATIONS

There are five organizations in the United States which register cats. Under the rules of the largest of these, two registers are kept, the Stud Book and the Foundation Record. The Stud Book is for cats of known ancestry through four generations, and the Foundation Record is for cats with less than four generations of traceable ancestry. The registrations are easily recognized, for registrations in the Stud Book contain the letters "S B" in the number, as "88SB888." The Foundation Record also shows as "88FR888." By this sign you may know whether the kit has a pedigree which will enable you to do scientific and wise breeding.

When you visit a cattery or a home where Siamese are raised,

don't come to a snap judgement on the cats just because they do not fawn on you or welcome your attempts to pick them up. You are a stranger, and, like children, the cats will sometimes be rather shy. Sit quietly and let them investigate you and decide that you are harmless. They'll know where you've been, what other cats you've seen, and what pets you have at home if they are given a few minutes to sniff you over. If you are looking for a pet kitten, then the one of a litter, even though it be the cull of the litter, which shows a decided liking for you, is the one you should take. He has decided that you are his ideal of what a human should be, and he'll love you all his life.

CHOOSING YOUR KITTEN

I remember one case in particular of a kitten choosing its own new master. A very nice young couple came here looking for a male kitten for a pet. There were two litters here at the time, and the male kit was in the younger litter, which meant a wait of three or four weeks before he could be removed to his new home. The customers decided upon the kit and stayed awhile to talk and arrange the time to come back for their baby after he had had his inoculations and been neutered. While we chatted, a little female from the older litter followed the man about, and each time he stopped moving she climbed onto the toe of his shoe and sat there contentedly. She was so persistent about it, and so obviously smitten with the gentleman that he and his wife decided that they'd better have two kittens instead of just the one. It's always pleasing to a breeder to see two kits go together, company for each other, and double enjoyment for the new owners.

Unless the buyer has considerable knowledge of Siamese, he must be guided to a great extent by the breeder of the kits from which he hopes to get a prospective winner. The different strains of breeding stock vary greatly in their development, and only the breeder who has seen previous litters grow can tell what the kittens will be at maturity.

Many buyers will insist that a kitten have a pale coat. The pale coat is pretty, but it is no guarantee that the kit, when it reaches maturity, will have the desired light coat. If the pigmentation is extremely light throughout, then the points will not be dark enough, nor do you have the expectation of the dark eye, which is so desired in the Siamese. The kittens which have rather "smutty" coats when small are much more apt to develop into well-colored adults with pigmentation even in coat, points, and eyes. Surprisingly enough, these dirty-coated kits will often show a fairly light coat which carries fairly consistently through their adult lives. Here again, you must be advised by the breeder, who has watched kits of the same breeding develop before, and who knows what color the majority of the cats of the particular breeding will carry.

WHAT TO LOOK FOR

The health of a kitten may be judged by his appearance, texture of coat, brightness of eye, and general liveliness. If the haws or inner lids of the eyes stay partly across the iris, the coat is open, or tacky, or the kit sluggish in action, avoid him, for these are signs of illness or generally poor condition. A general debility at an early age makes a kit a poor prospect for future enjoyment. The kit should feel weighty and solid for his size, as a friend so aptly put it, like a paperweight, small but heavy in proportion to his size.

Please, if you have visited where there have been any sick cats, or if you have recently lost a cat yourself, do not visit catteries or homes where Siamese or other purebred cats are being raised. There is nothing more disheartening to a breeder than to have some pleasant visitor explain, after half an hour of handling the cats and kits, that only days or weeks before, he lost a cat "by poisoning" (the amateur's common explanation for infectious enteritis, of which he knows nothing), or that he recently saw Mrs. So-and-So's cats, and "Gee, they all had the sniffles!" The poor breeder then spends two weeks watching anxiously for signs of illness among her own precious charges, all the while cursing the day the "pleasant" caller darkened her door.

Let us assume that you have developed such an admiration for the Siamese cat that you wish to purchase a queen and start breeding cats. In such a case, you will want the best available kitten, both from the standpoint of pedigree, and, if possible, in herself. You will, then, approach some leading breeder in the effort to procure a choice kitten, the "pick of the litter," as we say. But, if upon searching for some time, you find that breeders have previous commitments, and that the best kit of the litter is bespoken, do not hesitate to take the second best female kit. She may not win shows for you, but she will give you the same bloodlines to work with as her better sister, and

When you buy a Siamese kitten make certain that the youngster is in the best of health, well fed and well raised up to the time of your purchase. The kit should be playful, bright, and lively.

out of her you may, with just as good chance as the owner of the best kitten, get that perfect Siamese which will clean up the shows and give you a name as a breeder of really good cats. Better the poorest kit of a fine lot than the best of a poor lot.

A kitten's head at birth has a decided identation about the skull, and to my mind, the deeper this "dent," the typier the head will be when development is finished. As the kit grows, up to about four to five months of age, the top of the skull seems to push upward, with a domelike effect. This roundness flattens as the kit grows, all the height of the skull finally adding to the length. In proportion, as nearly as we have been able to come to perfection, the head is divisible by three: one-third from back of skull to space between the front of ears,

A litter of healthy, Seal-Point kittens at Ebon Mask cattery. These kits were just three-and-a-half weeks old when they posed for this, their first picture.

Mama proudly displays her two offspring . . . Seal-Point Siamese all.

one-third from that point to the top of the nose, and the remaining third from the eyes to the tip of muzzle. The head is approximately one and one-third times as long as it is wide at the widest point, across the top of the skull.

The kitten's neck should be noticeable, and the head not appear as if fastened directly down on the shoulders, but well separated from the body by a rather slender-looking neck.

Ears of the Siamese are large, upright, and wide-open at the base, with very little hair showing inside the ear.

The body of the Siamese, even of a three-months-old kitten, appears long—"svelte" is the term used in the standard, and it covers the type well. Legs are rather long, well-turned, not sticklike in appearance, and the hind legs slightly longer than the forelegs, giving the body an upward slant towards the rump. Feet should be small and oval, the second toe longer than the rest.

The tail should be long and tapering from the base to the tip.

Ideally, the tail should equal in length, the length of the body from the base of the spine to the spot between the shoulder blades. While the straight tail is the ideal, the kink is so common that allowance is made for it in the standard for judging. The kink should be at the very end of the tail, if it appears; and any malformation halfway up the tail, screwed tails, or short tails are grounds for disqualification in the judging ring.

We must emphasize the importance of the eyes in Siamese. Twenty of the one hundred points of the standard are given for proper eye shape and color. In shape the eye should be "oriental," slanting towards the nose, the inner edge of the upper lid cutting across the inner corner of the eye, and the outer corner of the eye much higher than the inner corner, giving the proper slanted look to the eye.

The color called for in the standard is "sapphire blue." As you know, there are sapphires and sapphires, but the true oriental sapphire is a deep, vivid blue, and this is the color the breeders strive to produce in the Siamese. Eye color in kittens is difficult for the novice to evaluate. In many lines of breeding, especially in those of concentrated English stock, there often appears an eye which contains two distinct rings of color, very deep next to the pupil of the eye, much lighter in the outer edge of the iris. These eyes take a long time to develop the color completely, sometimes, as in our own Doneraile Drusilla and Amdos Yankee, nearly two years. The darker ring in the center of the eye gradually spreads until the entire iris is the same even deep-blue, and eyes which develop in this way are almost without fail brilliant, never dull.

Some lines of breeding produce kittens which show the deep sapphire-blue eye from the first time when the eye color is noticeable, at about three to four weeks of age. To my mind, thinking of these kits, the name "Bedale" comes automatically, the Bedale prefix denoting those fine cats bred by the late Mrs. Wade, of England. These amazingly deep eyes retain their color throughout the life of the cat, varying seldom, even during illness. The color is deep and has great brilliance, almost as if a light shone in the eyes.

If a kitten has a pale sky-blue eye, with no variation in the color over the entire iris, do not look for improvement in the eye color as the kit matures, for it will not come. Any hint of green is a fault, and the eye should not appear purplish in tone either, but a clear blue.

With this much knowledge of what Siamese kittens should be, you

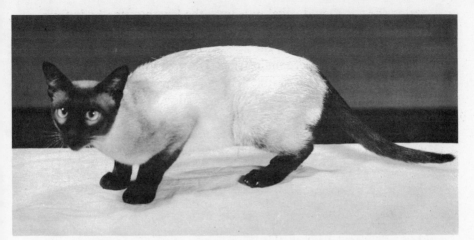

The imported, Seal-Point female, Doneraile Delia, bred by Mrs. K. R. Williams, and owned by Mr. and Mrs. Howard Stevens, Tucson, Arizona.

can pretty well judge for yourself whether a kitten is a future prospect for the show ring, or is just a nice young cat. But, you must almost always rely upon the judgement of the breeder, unless you have had many years of experience as a breeder yourself and know the various outstanding lines of breeding in the Siamese. There is a subtlety in the conformation of the Siamese which takes an experienced observer to see. Do not rush out and buy the first kitten you see, but look about, talk to many breeders, examining the kittens of different lines of breeding, and thus gain for yourself a more advantageous viewpoint, and through this knowledge you will be better able to plan future breeding which will produce better Siamese.

Siamese kittens, born white, gradually change color as they grow toward maturity, developing normal Siamese markings in the process.

CHAPTER 4

CARE OF THE NEW KITTEN

THE time has arrived when you are to get your "new baby," the Siamese, and excitement is running high in your home, especially if there are children in the family. It is always best to have a carrier of some sort for transporting the kitten, and since you will need one for future use anyway, now is as good a time as any to purchase or to make one.

CARRIERS

Carriers come in all sizes, shapes and materials, ranging from wood to plastic. A good fiber carrier, which is my own favorite, large enough for one good-sized cat to use on a trip, or for two animals for shorter distances, will cost about seven to ten dollars, depending upon details in construction. The advantage of the fiber carrier is that it is light in weight and warm. Wooden carriers are fine, but heavy to carry or ship, and weight does entail extra expense in shipping. Of late years, the plastic carriers, of a transparent material with metal bases and corners, are very popular and are used by many breeders who take cats long distances to shows. Carriers also can be purchased which are made entirely of airplane-weight aluminium, with provision for removal of sanitary trays, and insertion of feeding dishes without necessitating the opening of the carrier. Woven hampers are not too common in America but are used widely abroad. In cold weather these must be wrapped with brown paper to prevent chilling the occupant. A solidly-built carrier should have air-holes or screened windows at the ends, and the windows should have a curtain which can be rolled up or snapped down, depending upon weather conditions. Your pet shop usually has a complete line of carriers and catalogs from which you may select one to suit your taste.

When a breeder ships a kitten, the carrier should be large enough to provide a space for a sleeping section and room for a sanitary pan. A high carrier may contain a shelf for the kitten to sleep on, leaving the floor for exercise and pan.

Several layers of paper in the bottom of a carrier in which you are to transport the kitten from the breeder's home to your own place

Cat carriers; one for a fully grown animal and the other smaller, for a kitten.

will keep the baby warm, especially if a soft piece of blanket is placed over the papers.

THE KITTEN AT HOME

Do prepare a place for the kitten before you bring him home. It is upsetting for him to be just unceremoniously turned loose in a strange house and is apt to lead to nervousness and accidents following upon this condition. A quiet room with glass doors, perhaps, from which he can observe the activities of the household while still feeling protected, will serve admirably. Make sure he knows where his sanitary pan is located, and decide beforehand where you wish to keep it permanently, for if you change its location he may become confused. If the breeder has trained him to paper in the pan use that, and if you prefer something else, such as one of the fine sanitary products produced for just such purpose, make the change gradually. Sprinkle a little on top of the paper in the pan, and increase the amount from day to day until he becomes used to it and accepts it without fuss. The advantage of the litter materials is that the kit can dig in them, and they need be changed far less often than paper; but they do have the disadvantage of being tracked about the floors by the cat's feet. Watch the baby carefully for the first few days; make sure that he visits his pan at frequent intervals. In this way he will soon learn where he is expected to perform his functions and you'll have no trouble with dirtiness about the house. A device breeders sometimes use is to wrap up a piece of paper from the kitten's pan and send it along to be put in the pan in his new home. He quickly gets the idea and does not regard the new accommodations as strange.

Should there be other pets, especially dogs, do not expose the new baby immediately to their doubtful mercies. If he can watch them for a time and become used to their ways without shock, he will soon adjust to their presence. Nearly all Siamese learn to live in complete harmony with dogs. Some breeders keep a dog about so that kits become accustomed to the canines from birth, but I do not keep a dog for reasons which will be explained later in this book.

SIAMESE KIT AND SHEPHERD

I shall never forget when our first Siamese, then about three months of age, met our dog, a huge German Shepherd who was a friendly amiable sort, sweet and affectionate and still convinced, at nine years, that he was a lapdog! He was seldom in the house during the day, for he had his social calls to make all about the neighborhood and was warmly welcomed in most places. For the first few nights that the kitten was here I confined the dog to the cellar, so that she saw and heard him only from afar. About a week after Baby came to us I went to let the Boy up for his breakfast and Baby followed me to the cellar door in the kitchen. When I realized that she was at my heels I opened the door very slowly for about an inch and the dog shoved his nose into the opening sniffing wildly to see what was forthcoming for breakfast. He must have been surprised when the first thing his nose met was the nose of a Siamese kitten! Poor Baby, she was so amazed and scared she tried to go off in all directions at once, her feet whirling like the blades of a windmill as she sought traction on the slippery linoleum floor! It was three hours before she came out of hiding from under the living-room divan; but since I am firm believer in allowing my pets to take their own time about such things, she was left there in peace until she was ready to face the world with her fur smoothed down. But it wasn't a week before she was muscling in on his dinner, a noble effort but rather futile since he just put his face over the dish, made a noise like a vacuum cleaner, and the dish was empty! They were soon sleeping together, Baby pushing up against his heavy fur for warmth and complaining until he got into a position in which she could be comfortable. When the dog died about a year later, Baby looked everywhere for him and missed him tremendously, but since she was expecting kittens at the time I didn't get another dog and have not had once since.

CHILDREN AND KITS

If there are small children in the family, the trust of a young animal is the finest of training for them. Let the children feed the kitten and care for him, teaching them to be always gentle and considerate of the kitten's feelings, and they'll grow up with an attitude of thoughtfulness towards all God's dumb creatures. The child who has never enjoyed responsibility for, or trust of, an animal has missed one of the best experiences of his life. Nothing is more distressing to see, nor more of

Siamese cat and German Shepherd dog pal, giving the lie to the old adage about cats and dogs.

A Siamese cat is the ideal companion and playmate for young people (of all ages, I might add).

a reflection upon the parents, than the sight of a small child mauling or abusing a defenseless, tiny animal. Children learn by example and experience.

FEEDING THE KITTEN

The breeder will furnish you with a diet list for feeding the kitten. It is wise to follow this as closely as possible, making changes slowly so as not to upset the kit's stomach. There are a number of basic foods which all animals find acceptable, and if one is not available, another will be accepted.

Fresh, lean meat should be the main staple of any cat's diet. Horsemeat is quite good, provided it is lean; and, of course, if expense is no object, lean beef is ideal. Fresh, boiled white fish, well boned; chicken or fowl, well cooked and boned; rabbit meat, common in some parts of the country and relished by cats; canned beef or horsemeat and canned fish are all suitable.

Here I feel it is time to speak about diet for Siamese as apart from other felines. As a breed Siamese are notoriously deficient in calcium, and the diet must provide plenty of this necessary element for stronger bones and teeth. Also, since many Siamese show a definite allergy to fat—it is the only suitable term to explain the reaction of the Siamese to some substances—I feel it is necessary to stress the point of feeding lean meats and fat-free milk products. Here at Ebon Mask Cattery, kittens are weaned on skim milk diluted with warm water, and, as soon as they are ready to accept, solids fortified with fine-curd cottage cheese, several pounds of which are fed to our cats each week. One must judge the need of a fat-free diet by watching the reactions of the kits to each food as it is presented and taken. If one gives whole milk or canned milk and the kits show any looseness of bowels, skim milk or cottage cheese should be substituted for the whole milk. If the owner persists in feeding fatty foods, the kit will become upset and the bowel feces show a greyish and pale color, an almost sure sign of a liver upset, which also, of course, involves the production of bile for digestion.

We mix the cottage cheese with dry, prepared rice, baby cereal or farina, though for small kits I prefer the rice since it is so smooth and fine that their stomachs accept it readily. By adding hot water to the rice cereal and cottage cheese, one gets a smooth and nicely sloppy mixture which all the cats seem to enjoy. This is also one good way to

Vitamin and mineral supplements can be mixed in with the food or given separately with an eye-dropper as the administering vehicle.

see that the kits and cats get a good supply of liquids in the diet, if some of them are not "drinkers."

Our method of acquainting the babies with meat is to allow them to be with the queen when she is fed her main meals, and we find that when the kits show an interest in her food, they are ready for it. We have all meat, for feeding to the cats, chopped finely, and so it is quite suitable for the babies as well as for their mother. Here again, we take advantage of the opportunity and give liquids, warming the meat by adding very hot water to it instead of cooking it. The queen during periods of gestation and nursing gets a tablet consisting of a calcium concentrate with vitamin D added in her food each day, and when the kits begin eating with her, an extra tablet is added. Just crush the tablet into powder and mix with the meat. Our cats have never objected to it in any way since it is tasteless and not gritty.

When the kits are eating apart from the queen we give a concentrated fish liver oil with added vitamins A and D and mineral traces, three times a week in place of the tablet to provide vitamin A and phosphorus, for without these calcium is not readily assimilated. There seems to be a connection between all these vitamins and minerals, and one without the others does little good.

Horsemeat is a good source of protein, but has one serious lack. The fat of horsemeat is not assimilated by the cat's system, but is thrown off like a dose of mineral oil. Beef fat is readily absorbed, and for most cats some beef fat added to the horsemeat is good, once in awhile. Chicken fat is almost too readily accepted by the kittens' systems. If the kits have a little chicken broth with some yellow fat floating on the surface, inside of a half-hour one can see the fur become tacky and oily in appearance.

Kuan Yin's Rococo, Chocolate male son of Champion Lamar's Rococo. Bred and owned by Mrs. Adele Deeths, San Rafael, California.

Eggs are an excellent source of protein, but be cautious when introducing eggs to the diet; feed only a tiny bit of egg yolk to start and if no untoward symptoms occur, increase the amount each time. The white of egg has no real food value for the cat and is apt to be indigestible. We have never cared to feed lamb to the cats often, for it is inclined to be a greasy meat and often disagrees with them.

Some breeders feed vegetables to the cats, but we have never made a practice of this since a cat's intestinal tract is geared to meat, not roughage. One cat, some years ago, had a passionate fondness for stringbeans, and I gave her some whenever we had them at our own table. Any vegetable given a cat should be chopped very fine or strained to break down the fibrous matter.

Breads, especially rye bread, do not harm cats, and the unrefined and dark grains are a good source of vitamin B. A crust of bread is often put on the dishes for the studs, and they enjoy chewing these crusts, which helps clean their teeth and prevents formation of tartar next to the gums. I have had only one cat who has had tooth trouble, and she was eleven years old when she had to have several infected teeth removed; so I feel that diet and plenty of calcium do have a definite bearing upon this as well as upon general good health and muscle tone.

Sweets are not for cats, though once in awhile you will meet a cat who loves candy. Our Ch. H.R.H. of Ebon Mask, when he was a young lad in the days before he graduated to stud quarters, loved candy and would steal a piece of penuche, brown sugar fudge, and eat it all over the house—leaving a trail of sugar crumbs behind.

Fresh milk is a food we have not found very successful, for it seems most Siamese have a sensitivity to it, and unfortunately it causes diarrhea. Evaporated milk, mixed one-half to two-thirds with

Amdos Caduceus, Seal-Point, three month old male kitten, bred by Mme. A. M. D'Ollone and owned by Mrs. S. S. Nelson.

warm water, serves well as a substitute, as long as the cat can tolerate the fat content of the milk. Evaporated milk has a much finer curd than fresh whole milk; digestion is more rapid and much easier on the cat's stomach, particularly in the case of a kitten.

A well-fed cat is a contented cat and does not, usually, go searching about for bits to eat all the time. A balanced diet will bring a cat into good condition, keep his coat fine, silky and smooth, and maintain good muscle tone. Much depends upon proper feeding of the queen while she is carrying her kittens and nursing them. Serious deficiencies in her diet at these times will definitely affect her babies. If she is well-fed and has a sufficiency of calcium her babies will be hale and hearty.

Bringing up a Siamese kitten to adulthood is not very difficult. Use the same sort of common sense as with a human baby, and if the kit does not seem well, or is not as lively as usual, watch awhile and

Kittens in a basket. Young hopefuls, bred and raised by a knowledgeable breeder for future show competition.

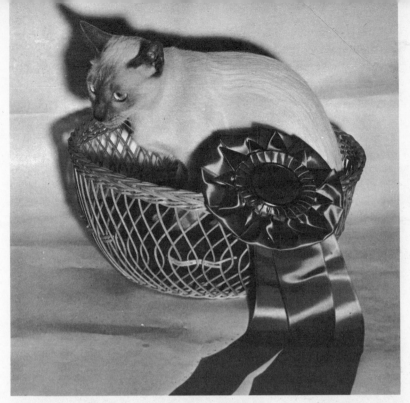

The end result of thoughtful breeding and care . . . you hope. This is Champion Montecito Darpi-Dell of Glory-S, Frost (Lilac) Point female, after being awarded the show rosette for Best of Opposite Sex. Bred by Mr. and Mrs. F. W. Burke and owned by Mr. and Mrs. William P. Scott of the Glory-S Cattery, Tujunga, California.

if the condition persists, take the kit to a veterinarian for a check-up.

We must realize that the Siamese is a highly-bred creature, and as a result is a rather nervous and intelligent animal. He needs exercise, good food, fresh air—in moderation, but not to excess—warm sleeping quarters, and a generally comfortable but not dull existence.

All of your cat's necessities—horsemeat, vitamins and supplements, canned foods, sanitary products, carriers and toys—can be found in wide variety in your local pet shop.

Double Champion Vee Roi's Bonnie Jean, Blue-Point female, on left. Her handsome companion is Double Champion Vee Roi's Krisadon, a fine Seal-Point male. The proud breeder-owner is Mrs. R. H. Hecht.

CHAPTER 5

SIAMESE QUEENS AND STUD CATS

TIME TO BREED QUEENS

THE Siamese queen may call as early as six or seven months of age, but mating at so early an age is inadvisable, for the development of the cat is not matured to a point where she is apt to carry and deliver her kits successfully. Ten months is about as early as a queen should be mated; this will bring her past her first birthday before the kits are born. However, if a queen calls persistently, it is sometimes necessary to mate her at an earlier age. Continuous calling may bring about a condition of hysteria, or the development of uterine cysts, affecting her breeding capacities in the future. The duration of periods of heat varies in different cats. Some may call only once a month, or even once in two or three months, and the period of actual "calling" may be only three to five days long, but it is not unknown for queens to keep calling for weeks on end, and to rest only a few days between periods of heat. Our Petita was only six months of age when she called the first time, and from then on she called for six days at a time, having rest periods of only two days between spells. We were forced, in order to protect her from actual damage, to mate her at nine months, when she was still very small (her name explains her size and type, I think) but she delivered three kittens after a rather hard, but not dangerous labor. She subsequently had nine litters, making ten in all, and never had the slightest trouble until, with the advent of a very large kitten who blocked the pelvis, she had to undergo a Caesarean to deliver her tenth litter. At normal size, neither fat nor skinny, Petita weighed a trifle under four pounds, so you can see, it does not take a large cat to make a good breeding queen.

TYPE OF STUD

It is important not only to choose a male with the required strength in type, but it is also necessary that one have some knowledge of pedigree so that he may know whether the ancestors of the particular cat also carry the wanted type. If the male is simply an individual, a sport in type, not like those in his background, there is a good possibility that he will not be prepotent in the type items looked for. In order to be potent in throwing type to his offspring, a male must carry, through the four generations, shown on his pedigree, strong indications of the length of head, or the body type, in the majority of the cats who form his ancestry. Do not hesitate to ask the owner of a stud for information about the pedigree and the cats appearing in it, for most stud owners are proud of their cats and ready to offer information upon request, to show that the stud should be able to give what is needed.

THE FEMALE'S "CALL"

I've had novices ask how one can tell when the female is in "heat" or "calling," and the answer to this is that you can't mistake it!

Petita of Ebon Mask and her kittens. The kits, at the time of this photograph, were four days old and had been delivered by caesarian section.

Four days before her litter was born and lovely in her coming maternity, the Seal-Point matron, Champion Chirn Sa-Hai Hansa poses for her breeder-owner, Mrs. Beth O'Donovan, of South Miami, Florida.

The call of the Siamese female has to be heard to be believed, and is so loud that unless one lives in a single dwelling, or has a regular cattery, it can pose problems. Along with the screaming there are physical signs: restlessness, the cat acting as if she itches, she washes herself constantly, twitches all over, rolls about the floor, and "scrambles" about, her front quarters down low and hind legs kicking out backward, a sort of crawl in reverse. The average is about five to seven days for this period of heat, and by the end of the time, one wonders how one small animal can keep up such a racket without entirely losing her "voice" or how such volume can issue from so tiny a sound-box.

It is, ordinarily, eight weeks or more after delivery before the queen will call again, but it is not unknown, though much commoner among domestic cats, for a queen to come in heat two weeks or less after the birth of the kittens. The queen should not, of course, be bred at this time for she is still nursing her kittens and pregnancy would affect her milk and cause upsets in the small kittens. It is best,

The pregnant Queen must be fed well to nourish the kittens forming within her.

if the cat can be restrained, to space breedings out so that not more than two litters a year are born. But, it is better to breed the cat more frequently than to have her ruined by persistent calling.

Assuming that you have a young queen of good breeding, and that your aim is to mate her to produce even better than she herself is, you must search for a stud who has whatever qualities you wish to intensify or improve in the queen. If the queen has good body type and color, but lacks somewhat in length of head, then your problem is to find a male who excels in that characteristic, being also good in general conformation, so as not to pull down the fine body type the queen has.

THE STUD SIAMESE

There are many fine males in this country today, of American breeding as well as imported stock. You would be well advised to visit the shows in the large cities and to study the show records and advertisements in the magazines devoted to pets. Owners of studs will readily furnish information about the studs, their strong qualities, prepotency as sires, weak points, too, so that you may be able to decide what to do.

Stud fees range from ten dollars to one hundred dollars, the average being from twenty-five to fifty dollars. In this, as in all else, one gets what one pays for, and true quality does not come at bargain prices. Fees are set according to the value the owner places upon the stud, depending upon the breeding, the show record, and the siring capabilities of the male. Also, the price may be set fairly high to discourage, tactfully, the use of the stud to sire kittens by mediocre females. The owner of the stud is anxious that the offspring of the male do him credit, and has no wish, unless he is very mercenary, to have him sire poor kittens. Unless the queen is of good breeding, the burden of producing good kits falls too much upon the stud, which is unfair. One must not expect miracles.

Some males are very prepotent, and to the experienced breeder, his trade-mark upon his offspring, to the third and fourth genera-

Here is a prime example of prepotency. Note the similarity in type between these two cats. The Siamese in the inset is the Seal-Point male, Ch. Millbrook's Moonshee, bred and owned by Mr. and Mrs. Walter Roose, North Haven, Connecticut. The larger photo is of Ch. Cuthpa D'Ista, a Seal-Point female bred and owned by Mrs. R. M. Cuthbertson, Lufkin, Texas. Both these cats are great-grandchildren of the same stud, but out of differently bred females, proving the genetic dominance of that specific third-generation-back male.

tions is visible. The head type thrown by some males is recognized everywhere, and other good males have produced hundreds of kittens, all of them showing remarkable type and color, while certain eye color and shape are directly traceable to one very fine male of some years ago. Prepotency is much to be desired in a stud cat, for it tends to distinctly improve each successive generation.

SHIPPING THE QUEEN

When you have investigated and decided upon which male you wish to have sire by your queen, you then write or visit the owner of the stud to make arrangements for service when the queen is ready. Here I offer advice to the novice to please NOT wait until the queen is calling to start looking about for a stud, for you may not have time to do the necessary investigating after she really starts calling. In self defense you may have to rush her to the nearest male, and he may not be at all what you really want, and you will suffer disappointment when the kits do not turn as out well as you hoped. All expenses of shipping the queen, or of communications regarding her visit, fall upon her owner, NOT upon the owner of the stud. The stud fee pays for the services of the male only, and is not returnable. If the cats mated, the male earned his fee, and most stud owners do not ask for fees in advance, only when the owner comes to take the queen home or before she is shipped back to her owner. Some stud owners will meet the queen at the nearest rail station or at the nearest airport, but this must all be decided upon and settled before the queen is shipped. The owner of the queen should provide her with a warm, safe carrier for traveling, and never ship a cat in anything that can damage easily or from which she can escape. One hears of females shipped in cartons or materials no stronger than cardboard, but the owner who cares about his cat will provide her with suitable accommodations for shipping as well as for her home surroundings.

Never, never ship a cat to a stud without first calling the owner to discover whether it is convenient for him to take your cat at the time. The stud could have another visitor, you know, or there might be illness, in which case the owner of the stud would not put the male at service for a time, until all danger of infection was past.

Be sure, positive, that your queen is in good health when you send her to a stud, with no signs of a cold, no dirty ears, or fleas. It is most unfair that the stud owner should have to combat illness after a visiting queen has brought infection to the stud house. If the queen is crossing state lines a certificate of health, issued by a veterinarian, should be attached to her carrier. Should the plane be grounded by bad weather, or the train delayed, the cat might have to be removed and the laws of some states require that the animal come from a "rabies free" area. Unless a certificate accompanies the cat you may find yourself billed for examination of the queen by a veterinarian.

Most air lines will not carry animals on passenger planes, except as part of a passenger's luggage. However, air-freight lines handle livestock well. A case in point—I have shipped kits from Boston to Jacksonville, Fla., the shipment leaving at 10:00 p.m., and arriving at 7:40 a.m. Fortunately, the kits seem to behave well enroute and to arrive in good condition, ready and eager to make friends with a new family.

On trips lasting twenty-four or fewer hours, I do not arrange for the kittens to be fed enroute, especially since fasting up to twenty-four hours does not harm them. I write a note that the carrier must not be set in the sun during warm weather or in a drafty place during cold weather, and fasten it to the carrier in plain sight. I have found the airline personnel to be co-operative and interested in the kits' welfare. I consider shipment by air much safer and speedier for cats than shipment by express. Their new owner should have all information concerning flight number, departure and arrival time, etc., well in advance of the actual receipt of the shipment, so that he may make suitable preparations.

THE STUD'S QUARTERS

Quarters for the stud should be roomy and sanitary. Extent of space depends, of course, upon location and circumstances. There are some very large catteries, one of which will be described and illustrated herein. A small stud house can still be efficient and comfortable for the animals, and I use our own as an example. We keep only the two studs, father and son, and their quarters take up about half of a two-car garage, a room about twelve by six feet with a seven-foot ceiling. Four cages, each six feet in length, double tiered, provide accommodations for the males and visitors. In one corner, at floor level, is an air vent with a sliding cover that can be regulated according to the temperature in this changeable New England climate. In the opposite corner, in the ceiling, is a circular air vent covered with screening so that the air which enters at one corner finds exit at the opposite and is forced to circulate through the quarters.

There is a shelf at the window (which is screened for summer weather), and the window is on the south side of the cattery, so there is plenty of sunshine in the cattery. Floors of the cages are wood, covered with vinyl flooring, easy to clean. Doors of cages are wide, the whole front of the cage being of wire mesh, half-inch size, with secure hooks to fasten the doors. Everything in the cattery is painted one solid color, either white or pale green, in high-gloss enamel, easy to keep clean, and provides a reflecting surface for the sunlight so that the cattery is cheerful. The heater is a fan type which blows air over a hot coil, all electric, which is certainly the safest form of heat for any animal quarters. The heater is set in an enclosure, open at the front, and it has grills that allow circulation but prevent curious paws from reaching into the heater and coming in contact with the blades of the fan. The heater is connected to a thermostat, which turns it on and off as the temperature rises and falls, and this keeps the cattery at an even 70 degrees throughout the winter. Insulation is in all walls and over the ceiling of the stud quarters, helping to keep the cattery cooler and more comfortable in summer and warmer in winter.

THE CATTERY

As an example of a larger cattery, where a large number of cats are kept, the Tang Wong Cattery of Seattle, Washington, is really fine. Architect-designed, it embodies everything for the comfort and well-being of the cats who live there, and for visitors.

For convenience, the cattery is connected to the house by the utility room and an enclosed porch. Through the center of the cattery runs a long aisle, with germicidal lamps at each end, and a ventilating fan to carry off stale air and provide proper circulation. The heat comes from radiant coils in the flooring, which is cement, and thus the heat always rises, and the floors are not chilly.

Shelves are provided for the cats for rest and exercise, while kittens are protected by off-floor pens, and warm places to cuddle until they are old enough to be allowed to climb about freely like their elders. Outside pens are accessible from the cattery by panels which slide

open, and sanitary pans may be changed through these panels too, or from inside the cattery, whichever is more convenient. Stud rooms are separated by solid wood-ply walls, or, if the walls are wire, the pen between is occupied by a queen, giving the boys something to think about besides each other—a very wise move.

Here, as in the case of the small stud house, one must consider the cost of maintenance and running it properly, for the expense is not inconsiderable and unless one is prepared to face it, one would be well advised not to go in for breeding, or at least not to keep studs. Studs must have separate quarters in almost all cases, for while they may be old love-bugs and gentle, they do have undesirable qualities.

Another view of the same cattery pictured above. This is an inside photo showing a play pen for cats and kittens and a kittening box, the lid of which remains closed until the kits are old enough to fend for themselves. The shelves, built high off the floor, are particularly favored by Siamese.

It is the great exception when a male is of such behavior that he may remain in the home without causing some inconvenience and distress to the people who have to live there too.

BREEDING

The queen, upon arrival at the stud quarters, should be caged by herself for a time, to adjust to strange surroundings, and to allow the stud to sing to her and to make himself attractive. We like to put her carrier in the cage with her so that she has something familiar from home. In this way she will be more at ease and feel less nervous.

After the queen has had time to become reconciled to her strange

A view of the cattery from the Stevens' house. Over the far door can be seen the germicidal lamp.

surroundings, she may be released in the stud house with the male. An active stud will not waste much time in mating the queen, but if she is extremely nervous, as maiden queens are apt to be, he may take some time to let her know he means her no harm, and she will eventually allow him to approach her without flying at him. The stud owner does not leave the cats alone together for any length of time, and never until he has witnessed the first mating, so that he may be sure the stud has earned his fee for services. We like to keep a queen two or three days, mating her on two successive days, in order to make sure, as far as possible, that the breeding will be successful. After the cats have mated, the female is very excited and is apt to attack the male viciously, so he should have a place to which he can jump to avoid her attack. A stool, small bench or shelf, upon which he can spring when the female leaps from him and turns upon him is really necessary. If the male is cornered, he will usually threaten to retaliate if she is too disagreeable, and sometimes will slap her hard to drive her away. But I have never known a male to really fight a female he has mated. Having the male marked or scarred is one of the risks the stud owner cannot avoid when a female comes for service, but after providing as well as possible for every contingency, he can only hope for the best.

The principal reason stud cats are not kept in the house is that they "spray." This has nothing to do with house training, but is just an evidence of the maleness of the stud. About one in fifty to a hundred males will make a suitable house cat, and even these have their moments. It is that old biological urge, the old "debbil sex" that makes the Toms spray and it is certainly nothing one would wish to live with. Frequent washing of the stud quarters, use of chlorophyll and small ultraviolet lamps are means of keeping down odor in the stud house, but it still lingers on! Thus, there are many who like to breed Siamese, but, because of the necessity for separate quarters, do not wish to keep male cats. It is a considerable expense to maintain proper stud housing, with heat, lighting, constant care, and repainting. Stud quarters need frequent sterilizing, especially after a queen has visited, and for this we use a large ultraviolet lamp, exposing walls, cages, floors, in fact, everything in the stud house, to its rays for periods of half an hour for several days. This kills airborne germs and also sterilizes all surfaces touched by the cats. Every precaution needs to be taken to protect the stud and visitors against infection. Keeping studs is really work, whether one does it himself or has help to care for the quarters, as some of the larger catteries do.

During the breeding seasons, heaviest in February and September, the stud needs his diet fortified with plenty of protein and vitamins, for if he becomes run-down, due to over-activity during the mating seasons, his offspring will reflect his lack of condition. We do not believe in using the studs too frequently, preferring to limit the stud to fewer matings, thus giving him every chance to produce the best of which he is capable. Beaten egg, plenty of fresh meat, fish and milk, if he tolerates it well, with added calcium and fish liver oils, will keep the stud in good condition. Calcium must be judiciously used with males, for they are prone to development of kidney or bladder gravel. Vitamin A helps to counteract this trouble and may be given with the fish-liver oils or in capsule form, separately. Sometimes one sees a male who is very nervous and high-strung, especially at the shows. These males usually respond well to additional calcium in the diet, given in fairly generous amounts over a period of a month or so. It is lack of this essential, in many cases, which causes these males to be so jittery.

When the female returns home after mating, keep her confined until after she is entirely over all signs of being in heat. Mating itself does not bring the "season" to an abrupt end, and even though the cat is bred she will probably call for the usual term. Should the cat not be bred and come in again, most stud owners are willing to give a return service free, but this must not be taken for granted, for it is not compulsory upon the stud owner to give this return service. It is really a favor upon his part, for, if the cats mated, the stud earned the fee and the owner has no further liability. It is well to inquire, when arranging to send the queen, whether the stud owner does give a return service in case the mating does not take, then there can be no ground for misunderstanding. The stud owner is naturally anxious that the mating be fruitful, for it is not good advertising for the stud that a mating did not produce. I have taken females back three times, allowing several matings upon each visit, in the attempt to give satisfaction to the owner of a queen. In some cases the queens are difficult to breed successfully, seeming to have only a short span during the heat when they will mate with results. Others will conceive with only one mating, so the stud owner, in order to insure success, usually allows mating on two days in order to provide a successful mating. Here it seems a good place to explain that in very rare cases are the studs responsible for failure of the female to conceive upon mating. Most stud owners have queens bred to the stud and carrying kittens, which proves his potency. The fault, if it can be called that, lies almost always in the female. There are so many things that can interfere with conception that it is useless to enter into the subject. Cysts in the ovaries or uterus are common and can often cause failure to conceive, or over-acid conditions of the blood can cause failure to conceive, or abortion of the kits at so early a stage that the owner does not even realize that the cat has aborted the litter.

It has often been said that a cat will conceive and fully germinate all the seed ready to be fertilized, and that double conceptions are impossible. This, according to what I have seen, is a fallacy, I know of a Siamese queen who lives with the stud, but they roam the grounds

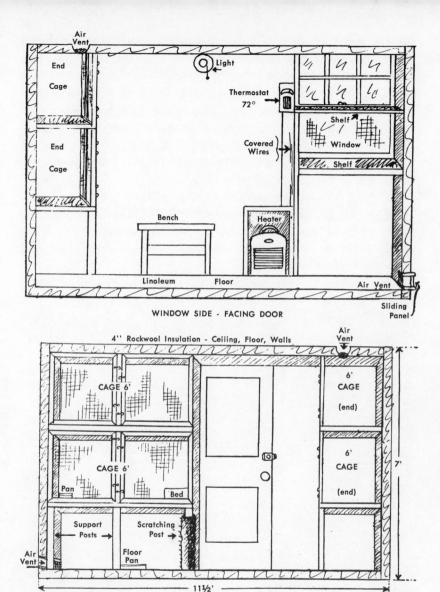

WINDOW SIDE - FACING DOOR

The diagram shows two walls of stud quarters designed to accomodate two males. The upper diagram illustrates the window side, facing the door, while the lower diagram depicts the opposite (or door) wall. All exposed surfaces are painted white and the floor is covered with linoleum.

loose, and the female mated with the barn cat, and afterwards with the Siamese male. She delivered a litter of four common kittens and one Siamese baby.

Novices often blame or credit the stud for the number of kittens in a litter, and this is not right. The female is responsible for the number of kittens, for that depends upon the number of eggs expelled by the ovaries at the time she is mated. A normal male with one mating will give enough active sperm to fertilize any number of eggs the female carries, be it one or twenty.

Lately, it is said that the sex of the babies is set by the male. Whether this is true I do not know*, but I do know that we seem to run to litters of females and litters of males, more often all one or the other, than mixed. The winter of 1953 produced seven males and only two females in three litters.

Do your best to keep the queen from over-activity during preg-

Champion Doneraile Brun Malvana, imported, Chocolate-Point female. Breeder, Mrs. Kathleen Williams, England; owner, Mrs. Rex Naugle. Primos, Pennsylvania.

*This is not true. The sex of the resulting progeny of any breeding is a matter of chance.

The cat on the left is a Blue-Point Siamese and its companion is a Red-Point Siamese. Together they make a handsome pair.

nancy to avoid the possibility of injury and abortion of the litter. High jumping is to be discouraged, if possible, and she should be provided with every encouragement to rest, eat well, but not too heavily, and to be nice and lazy during her term of pregnancy. Gestation is from sixty-three to sixty-six days, plus or minus one or two days, ordinarily, or about nine weeks. Heavy feeding during pregnancy will make the kittens large and the queen fat, both conditions leading to difficulty in delivery. The regular diet, fortified with added calcium and vitamins to provide good bone for the kittens, without robbing the queen will ensure her a good litter.

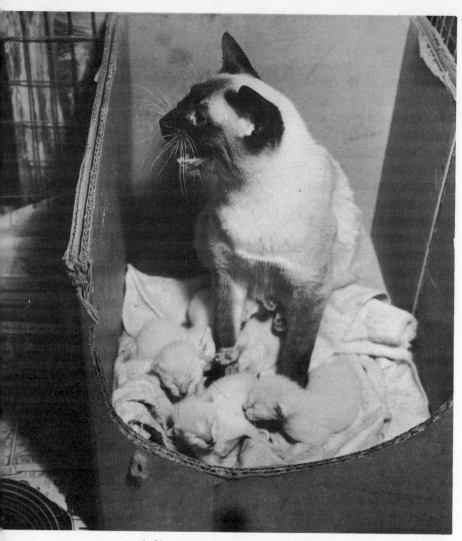

A Siamese and her brood. This fine female, through her litter of kittens, is fulfilling her destiny. Note the whiteness of the kits at this early age.

CHAPTER 6

PREGNANCY OF THE CAT

THE first noticeable sign of pregnancy in the Siamese Queen is a slight enlargement and increased pink pigmentation of the nipples. It is not, usually, until the fifth week or after, that one sees any increase in the size of the abdomen. The final weeks of gestation are the time when the kittens really grow, and it is to the advantage of the cat that she deliver at sixty-five or sixty-six days, not to go on to the sixty-nine or seventy days, for those extra days, few as they may seem, mean much added size in the kittens.

We have found, with few exceptions, that at the end of the sixty-fifth day, starting into the sixty-sixth day, the cat begins labor. As much as a day before labor actually begins, there may be a mucus discharge, thick and yellowish, but this is nothing to become alarmed about. It is a sign that nature is beginning preparations for the kittens' delivery, and that one had better stick pretty close to the house, not leave the queen alone for any length of time. No matter how many litters a female may have had with no trouble, there is always the chance that she may have difficulty, and I, for one, could never forgive myself if I left a queen to struggle through labor alone. Siamese do depend upon the owner for support and evidence of affection during any time of distress. They are rather super-civilized felines.

PREPARING FOR THE LITTER

About two to three weeks before the kits are due, one should plan a place for the queen to deliver the babies, a spot where she can be watched over, and helped if necessary. Dark closets and out-of-the way spots should be closed and put "out of bounds" from that time on. We, for years, have used a bottom drawer in a dresser as a maternity ward, and the cats like it, second, of course, to my bed. The drawer opened about half-way makes a rather cave-like spot, sheltered and dim, which suits the cats right down to the ground. Prepare the drawer with cotton sheet blankets (these are a wonderful help in such times, easy to launder, and soft and warm) and every time the queen follows you into the room, put her in the drawer for a moment, stroking her and talking to her the while, and she will come to accept this as a spot she may consider her own.

A day or so before the date the kits are due, get all your supplies together, and place them near the drawer where the kits will be born. Pieces of turkish toweling, clean and soft, a bottle of alcohol, scissors, and bottles to fill with hot water, or an electric pad—all these should be readily available.

When the queen starts in labor, she has a peculiar cry, never heard at any other time, plaintive and not very loud, a distress cry. You will recognize this cry easily, for it is very different from the ordinary tone of the cat's voice. The queen usually, if she is devoted to her owner, will follow her about, insisting upon sitting in her lap, all the while telling her that something out of the ordinary is going on, and why, oh, why, doesn't Lady Dear do something about it? I like to spend this time, until the kits are born, in the room where everything is prepared for the birth. The queen will soon go into the drawer and dig herself in under the blankets lining the drawer, coming out once in a while to see that the owner is standing by. Labor, with a first litter, may be prolonged, but usually is not too long with succeeding litters. After the first real contractions, which are easily seen and recognized, the cat should deliver the first kit within an hour or two. If hard contractions continue longer than that, with no sign of progress, it is advisable to call the veterinarian so that, if there is real trouble he will be standing ready to aid.

BIRTH OF THE KITTENS

In normal delivery, the kit should come head first through the birth canal, but tail-first deliveries are very common. The head delivery is easiest for the queen, for once the head has been passed, the kit's body follows quickly. Tail deliveries mean that the big rib cage must pass through the pelvis first, and this is more difficult than the passage of the head.

Each kitten is enveloped in a skin sack, transparent and filled with fluid. When the kitten starts through the birth canal, this sack sometimes is forced through first, the water forming a sort of blister-like protrusion before the kitten appears. Sometimes the force of the contractions makes the bubble very full of the fluid and keeps the progress of the kitten back. Should this occur, pinch the bubble, or sack, between the nails of thumb and first finger to break it and allow some of the "water" to escape, and the kitten will then come through rapidly as the pressure is relieved.

The kitten is attached to the uterus by the cord, or placenta, and this must follow the kitten, the afterbirth coming entirely free of the queen with each kitten. In the normal course of events, the queen will clean the kittens, eating the afterbirth and chewing the cord off close to the kitten's navel. Here it is best to explain, for those who are inexperienced in handling animals, that while this procedure may shock the sensitivities of some readers, it is an entirely instinctive process with the cat. You must realize that before the cat was a domesticated creature, when it lived in the wilds, she had to leave no trace of herself for any other animal to find. Hence, all traces of the birth of the young had to be destroyed and any sign of dirt buried, to escape notice of enemies.

Should the queen have difficulty in passing the kitten through the canal, when part of the body has been expelled, wrap your fingers in a piece of the turkish toweling, grasp the kitten's body firmly, and

Ch. Doneraile Drusilla, imported, and her two weeks old kittens.

69

A family portrait, Mom, Dad, and the kids.

as the queen bears down, with the contractions, ease the kitten free of the canal. Do not pull upward on the body of the kitten, nor pull hard, for either is apt to cause an umbilical hernia, not a dangerous condition in itself, but one that is unpleasant to see and which may require an operation to repair.

A queen delivering her first kitten sometimes seems very surprised to see what she has done and is a bit confused as to proper procedure with this odd wiggling creature. Leave the kit alone for a minute or two, to see whether the queen will not, of her own accord, start to wash the baby. One swipe of her rough tongue will break the sac in which the kit is enclosed and allow him air to breathe. Should she refuse to wash the kit, break the sac over the kitten's face, and then, again wait for a few minutes to give the queen a chance to take an interest in her offspring. Most queens will instinctively wash and clean the baby, but should she refuse, the job is up to you.

If you must take care of the kitten, cut the cord carefully about two or more inches from the kitten's body, holding the cord between thumb and first finger NEXT to the body, and cutting on the side

A Siamese mother feeding her fast growing youngsters.

AWAY from the body. Pinch the cord firmly, twisting and pressing it between the thumb and finger to prevent hemorrhage and bring normal bleeding to a stop. Your hands should, of course, have been washed in alcohol before you touch the new-born kitten. Take the kitten in a piece of the turkish toweling and massage it firmly, from the rump to shoulders, to encourage active breathing and to dry the baby off. When the queen takes care of the kit herself she washes it roughly, and this has the same effect as the massage you give when you care for the kitten.

In extreme cases, where the kitten does not come to and start breathing well, or when the kit seems blue and lifeless, one sometimes gets good results by dipping the kit into quite warm water, following this by dipping it into cold water, alternating the immersions. It induces a shock to the kitten's system and causes the baby to breathe convulsively. Once the kitten breathes strongly and cries out, as it will, dry it off and keep it warm either on a heating pad or in the nest of bottles.

Have a nest of hot water bottles ready, covered with a blanket, and place the kit in this nest, covering it with a corner of the blanket. If the queen shows interest, allow her to investigate the baby, but watch her closely, especially if it is her first litter, for new mother cats sometimes become extremely agitated and bite the kittens in their attempts to take them away from you. Here, again, your company and the sound of your voice all the time the cat is in labor help to keep her calm. Restrain her gently, if necessary, and remove the kit to a safe place outside the drawer. One advantage of using the large dresser drawer is that it allows room for the queen to move about while in labor, and still leaves room for the kittens' nest of bottles and blankets. When the queen starts in labor to deliver the next kitten, which may be a matter of minutes or an hour after the delivery of the first kit, she will lose interest in the one already born.

Here I wish to explain my reasons for not keeping a dog with the cats. The Siamese female is excitable and high-strung when she has young kits, especially at time of delivery and for a few days thereafter. The presence of a dog in the room or the noise of his barking in the house may prompt her to kill the kittens. This may sound strange, but one must realize that in the zoos when the lioness or tigress has young, great care is taken to prevent her being disturbed in any way, for she will kill her cubs if she feels that they are in any danger. The domesticated cat will do the same thing, and I have known of several cases where a female Siamese has killed her kits, and in each case, a dog was freely allowed to roam the house, and investigate the kits as he pleased. Tragedy was the result; hence, I advise that dogs be kept entirely apart from the female cat at kittening time.

CARE OF NEW-BORN KITS

The average number of kits in a litter is from three to six, but cats have sometimes only one, or as many as—and this I heard only recently—THIRTEEN! The kits are quite small, much smaller than the kittens of the domestic cat, but very active from birth. In profile the head resembles that of a lioness, long, and rather heavy appearing at the muzzle, with the top of the skull very clearly outlined by an indentation which encircles the top of the head just above the eyes. The head and body should appear long, and the tail skinny and tapered. The muzzle should not seem square, but taper from across the eyes to a rounded end at the mouth. The feet and legs are slim

The kittens grow fast, soon assuming markings, becoming individuals and showing the promise of their coming maturity.

and the feet look almost like little hands, the toes are so very well defined and bony at birth with the claws quite evident. Once the kit breathes well, and settles down, the skin becomes quite bright pink, showing this brightness especially on belly, nose and feet pads. This pinkness is a sign of good circulation, and once the kit shows this, your worries are over, for it proves that his heart action is good.

If a litter of four or five kits is delivered, the process may take as long as four to six hours, or may be over in a much shorter time. The strength of the queen, as well as the force of the contraction when she is in labor, govern the time the complete delivery will take.

When the last kitten has been born, the queen will settle down and wash herself thoroughly and show interest in the babies. Palpate her abdomen to encourage shrinking of the uterus and prevent hemorrhage. Make a good-sized nest of the water bottles, or the heating pad, and change the blankets in the drawer so that all will be clean and warm for her and her new family, and then, LEAVE HER ALONE for a couple of hours or more to rest and become acquainted with her children.

I never have bright lights in the room where the kits are born, but keep the room rather dim, even during delivery, for that is the way the queen likes it. If left to her own devices, she'll go where it is dark to deliver her kits, so I try to follow, as closely as possible, the condition she herself would choose and still allow convenience to aid her if help is needed.

COMPLICATIONS

If, when labor is well under way, there seems to be no progress after a couple of hours, it is wise to call the veterinarian for consultation. Three injections of one-fourth cc of Pituitrin at one-half hour intervals are often used to increase force of contractions. We had the experience with a queen who had had nine previous litters being unable to deliver her kits. I did not become alarmed until several hours had passed, for she had never before had any difficulty whatever in having her kittens. We took her to the vet's in the car, my husband and daughter (who was finishing her first year in nurses' training) along for moral support, since the queen was one especially dear to my heart, my own loved pet. Our good vet and his nurse wife took over, with my husband and daughter standing by to do what they could, and a Caesarean section was performed on the queen, while, the sissy I am, I paced the waiting-room floor, wringing my hands. A Caesarean is all right, if done by a truly competent surgeon, but it is nothing I would deliberately make an animal undergo. The source of Petita's trouble was a very large kitten, which had come normally, head first, but the head was so large and well developed that it became wedged in the pelvic circle and could not pass completely. This kit was, of course, dead, but four live kittens were delivered, three of which lived to grow up. They were limp and very white at birth, for her long labor had exhausted them as well as the mother. We massaged them, gave artificial respiration, timing the pressure on the ribs as closely as possible to their normal breathing rhythm, and even breathing into the mouth of one little fellow who was most reluctant to take up the burden of breathing for himself. Three of the kits were all right within ten to fifteen minutes, but the fourth, a very promising male kit, was a good half hour in becoming pink and lively like the others.

The incision for the Caesarean delivery was made on the side, just in front of the hip bone, and no bandages were used. Dissolving sutures were used for the stitches for closing the uterus and muscles and peritoneum, but the outside incision was fastened with tantalum wires. There were no stitches abscesses from these wire sutures, and when they were removed after a week, the incision line was hardly noticeable, and the fur grew back so well that one cannot see where the operation was performed. She nursed her kits quite successfully.

The queen was not bred again. Always there is danger that scar tissue resulting from a Caesarean section may rupture through being stretched or through being contracted at delivery—with probably fatal results. Since Tita has not come in heat again, we have not had her spayed. Even though a cat breeds normally up to her eighth or ninth year, following a Caesarean, she naturally rests for about eighteen months. Our Tita, nearly eight years old at that time, has enjoyed a peaceful and quite normal existence ever since.

DIET OF QUEEN

During the time the queen is carrying and nursing her kits, she needs a diet strong in calcium and vitamins, as well as strong in protein. Starches do nothing but add fat to the cat and make the kittens too large. Calcium, more than one would ordinarily give, allows the queen to give plenty of the necessary calcium for good

Siamese cats love to play together. This handsome pair mirror the ultimate results of good breeding.

bone structure to the kits without robbing her own system of this most necessary element. Do not overfeed, especially during the last two to three weeks of the pregnancy, for this will only make the queen fat and the kits large and delivery difficult. Maybe I've said this before, but it does need emphasis, for so many people think that one must feed the cat when she is pregnant as if she were eating for five instead of one. A slight increase in food intake is all right, but don't, please, overdo it. It is a mistaken kindness.

The queen will not show much interest in food for twelve hours or more after the kits are born, but place a dish of fresh cool water where she can get at it easily, perhaps in the far corner of the drawer or box in which she and the kittens are staying. When she is hungry she will let you know, and then give her a light meal of meat or cereal, whichever she shows preference for, and be sure that she gets her CALCIUM each and every day.

I suppose this chapter sounds as if a cat will easily do whatever you wish her to do and have the kits in the spot you choose, but sometimes one gets fooled. The same queen that had the Caesarean section, when she had a previous litter several years ago, chose her own spot and almost got away with it, even though I was right there. Petita always comes to bed with me to cuddle on my arm with her head on my pillow for a while, until I fall asleep. Her kits were due almost any time, but she had shown no signs of being ready to deliver them when we went to bed that night, and we settled down as usual. Along in the wee hours of the morning I woke with a start, something very hot against my hip. I turned on the light, without moving my body, and turned back the covers, and sure enough, WE had a kitten! Had I not wakened, I suppose she'd have had all five there and surprised me in the morning. Tita is a great talker, always "yaketa-yaketaing," and singing a song, but that night she never made a sound, quiet as a mouse, getting her own way, at least in part. The rest of the babies were born in the dresser drawer, properly, as they should have been. Only folks who have lived with Siamese can understand them, and those who have not lived with them, should, for they are missing a very interesting companionship.

Drusilla, when her last babies came, chose the doll carriage, which we have kept in the hall since our younger daughter outgrew her love for dolls. It's almost as big as a regular baby carriage and comes in very handy when young friends with small children come to visit, for we tuck the human babies into the carriage for naps.

I came downstairs in the morning, and Dru was sitting in the carriage, and I patted her and said "good morning" in passing and she never said a word. Ten minutes later, when I went to call my husband, there she was, with a new-born kitten in the carriage, just sitting looking at the baby! I wheeled the carriage out into the kitchen and between getting breakfast, husband off to work, and daughter off to school, supervised the birth of the rest of the litter, two more kittens. All did well, despite the informal arrangements!

Dimple asks to have her "tummy" rubbed for hours, sometimes even days, before the kittens are scheduled to arrive. A very long-bodied, graceful, and slim cat, she has her kittens as easily as "falling off a log"! Nevertheless, she fusses far more than Galatea, who has a much more trying time. Even on the several occasions on which Dimple delivered but one kitten she demanded much attention and sympathy. It seems that Siamese in their smug satisfaction somehow or other manage to have matters to go *their* liking—whether *we* like it or not.

Delicate and soft in shade and truly feminine, this is
Dalai, a Red-Point female Siamese.

CHAPTER 7

HEALTH
OF KITTENS AND CATS

Approved by Pierre Morand, D.V.M.

SIAMESE kittens are, in the majority, strong and healthy, once they have passed the first few critical weeks of life. Due to their high breeding they are, of course, more highstrung and nervous than the ordinary domestic cat, but, due also to their breeding, they are more intelligent and affectionate, more devoted to man, than other felines. One does run into difficulty at times, and in this chapter I shall try to point out how to avoid some of the commoner pitfalls, and how to cure the less harmful troubles.

One cannot begin to offer advice comparable to that which the veterinarian, with his years of study and experience, is able to give, nor does one attempt to do so. The prescribing of medicines and the diagnosis of illness are the special province of the veterinarian. It does happen, however, that, just as with children, there are common ailments which the head of the home is expected to be able to care for. It is surprising how many of the illnesses of cats are like those of man, though they are not actually the same, nor are they transmissible, with a few exceptions. Nearly all animal sicknesses are too far down the scale to be transferred to man, but man can transmit his virus ailments and some actual germs to animals.

CARE OF EYES

One of the earliest illnesses seen in kittens is a condition of rheumy or sticky eyes. A cold can cause this or it may be due to a lack of vitamin A, and of vitamin D. In this case one gives fish liver oil fortified with viosterol; preferably, in the case of kittens, in concentrated form, the dose being two drops a day for several weeks. This is a fairly heavy dosage, and it would be wise to watch the kittens closely and to decrease the dose to one drop if there are any unfavorable signs. If the queen has had plenty of vitamin fortification in her diet during pregnancy the kits will not suffer this disability. Lack of vitamin A brings about a weakness of the eyes and the inability to stand light in the eyes, (photophobia), while lack of vitamin D makes the kits subject to catching cold easily. Two drops of the concentrated oil is the equivalent of a full teaspoonful of the more mildly refined fish liver oils.

If a cold is the cause of the eye condition, penicillin ophthalmic ointment usually brings quick relief, along with general care for cure of the infection. Here I must warn of a condition sometimes caused by injection of penicillin intramuscularly, and the local application of penicillin base salves. It happens, though not commonly, that a person or an animal may set up a sort of allergy to the surface application of penicillin if the same drug is used in injections. Should this happen to be the case with a kitten or cat being treated for a cold and eye inflammation, the inflammatory condition of the eye will become much worse with the application of the penicillin ophthalmic ointment. I would suggest, in the case of penicillin injections, that you use a sulfathiazole ointment for the eyes instead of the penicillin ointment under these circumstances. If you do use the penicillin in both instances, watch for reaction in the eyes and stop application of the ointment immediately if angry swelling or bloodshot appearance of the eye occurs. Application of warm saline solution (water, one pint; salt, one teaspoonful) may be soothing to the lids and will not harm the eye, or a warm boric acid solution (same proportions of water and powdered boric acid) will be beneficial.

Any injury to the surface of the eye, such as a scratch or the presence of foreign matter in the eye, will respond to penicillin ophthalmic ointment, and to washing with the boric acid wash. Clean pellets of cotton, a fresh one for each eye to prevent transmission of infection from one eye to the other, should be used. Soak cotton well in the boric solution, then squeeze gently over the eye, opening the lids to allow the liquid to run into the eye and over the surface of the eyeball. In using ointment, place some of the salve in the corner of the eye, and then press it gently against the lids, forcing the lids slightly open with the fingers. The ointment melts from the natural heat of the flesh, and thus enters into all parts of the eye. One can safely use either the ointment or the boric wash several times a day, for neither, by itself, sets up irration.

Sulfathiazole ophthalmic ointment is often prescribed, but some cats show a definite allergy towards sulfa drugs and one must watch for any such reaction, ceasing application immediately.

Siamese are hardy cats, but they, too, are subject to colds and sniffles. Treat the cold before it leads to more serious disease.

The eyes of Siamese kittens, due perhaps to their albinistic breeding, are extremely sensitive to light, and they should, therefore, be protected for the first three weeks from very bright lights. Do not expose them to direct sunlight nor to harsh electric light. They need not be kept in the dark, nor even in an extremely dusky room, but, just as one does with a child who has measles, one is careful that the room is not bright, but rather dim, the lights being shaded. The intensity of the light may be increased gradually after the first two weeks. The eyes open at any time after four days, but seldom take longer than ten days for complete opening. Sometimes kits are born with eyes already starting to open, or the eyes begin to open very shortly after birth. These kits need even more protection than the ones whose eyes take the normal length of days to open. The condition of having the eyes open at birth is not normal, and anything outside the norm is something to watch very closely. Infection during the birth is common in these cases, and should penicillin treatment not cure it completely, the kits are better put to sleep than allowed to survive to future blindness or weak sight.

CARE OF EARS

The most common ailment of the ears is the infestation of ear mites, which are tiny parasites, almost colorless and practically invisible to the human eye, but easily seen under slight magnification. These pests burrow into the deeper recesses of the ears and set up an irritation which, if neglected, can drive a cat mad and even result, due to secondary complications, in the cat's death. If your cat sits with ears pulled down and back, outward slanted, as if listening intently to some distant sound, and if he scratches at his ears, digging the hind paw into the ear or forcibly scratching at the outer base of the ear, he probably has mites. The surest sign of mites is the exudation of a crusty, dark, almost black wax from the ear, looking very dirty. The normal wax of a cat's ear is practically colorless and oily, a very pale brownish color and never obvious; more, I think, a lubrication than anything else. The blackish wax with the crusty appearance is never seen except when mites are present.

The great danger of mites is that they set up a condition of irritation which leads to inflammation and infection of the inner ear,

Clean your cat's ears periodically with a cotton-tipped swab. During the cleaning process any abnormal ear condition can be seen and treated.

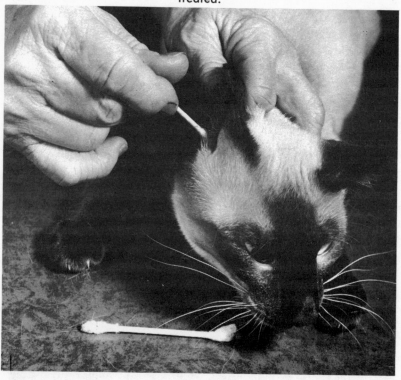

deep below the part that one can see. This in turn can lead to infections of the nasal and sinus passages, including the mastoids, and can, if neglected, kill the cat.

If the irritation is allowed to pass unnoticed for any length of time, the scratching which the cat does can injure the outer ear. Formation of blood clots in the tissues of the ear, or haematoma, may result. This often entails operative measures in and many cases leaves the ears crumpled, ruining the cat's appearance and ending any show prospects he may have had. Injury to the skin will leave a bare spot on which hair will not again grow, and this is considered a scar or deformity in judging.

The treatment for ear mites is not today the complicated or agonizing one of even a few years ago. If the case is not too stubborn or far progressed you may treat the ears at home, having obtained from the veterinarian a solution of rotenone in oil, which will easily kill the mites. If the case is deep-seated, you should have the veterinarian himself handle it at first, for the ears must be thoroughly cleaned deep down, with ether or alcohol, before application of the rotenone oil can be started. I prefer alcohol to ether for cleaning, because the ether dries the skin out far more than does the alcohol. Once the ears are cleaned, dip a cotton-wrapped small stick, or "Q-tip" as it is called, in the oil solution, and go deep down into the crevices of the ear, being careful not to bruise the skin inside the ear. Be sure the oil runs down into the ear, and wipe the inside surface of the upper ear and about the base of the ear on the outside with the swab. Use a clean swab for each ear. Three treatments a week for two weeks will usually bring the condition to a conclusion satisfactory to everyone except the mites! The rotenone is the same as that used to kill common garden pests, and mites are of the same species as the garden varieties. The rotenone does not harm the fur or cause it to fall off the ears. Bless the research man who discovered that rotenone is not harmful to cats! It is a far cry from the old "creosotish" medications which used to necessitate, in many cases, the anesthesia of the cat before treatment, the medicine was so violently painful.

CANKER OF THE EAR

Canker of the ear is a secondary complication caused by the infestation of mites. The canker is a sore spot in the ear which exudes a serum. This liquid forms a granular deposit as it drains from the ear and comes into the air. These deposits should be gently removed after softening them with warm boric acid solution, and the ears dusted with penicillin powder to cure infection. Cleanliness of the ears is truly important, for if the ears are kept clean, mites will not be able to propagate and so secondary infections may be avoided and the cat saved much unnecessary suffering.

ABSCESSES

Abscesses, whether of the ears or other parts of the body, are treated much alike. In cats, infections of the blood tend to localize, and real blood poisoning, as we know it in other animals and in humans, is rare. Abscesses of the cat's body usually break externally, releasing the poisons. Care entails washing frequently with a mild disinfectant. If the surface heals over before drainage is completed, it must be opened and the scabs kept off, so that free drainage results. In case the abscess does not break by itself, the veterinarian will open it by lancing, inserting a wick to assist drainage; and this must be kept free of scabs or dried serum, the surface washed several times a day. Though the treatment must cause some pain, a cat will not fight against the treatment. He seems to realize that you are trying to help him and will stand for a good deal of rough handling without protest.

BOWELS

Constipation is common among cats, and is sometimes a rather persistent condition. I do not advise indiscriminate dosing for this condition or for any other, but unless the condition is long-lasting and causes trouble, one can take measures to correct it without bothering the busy veterinarian and taking up his time with minor ailments. It is safe to give a dose of a teaspoonful of mineral oil three times a week for chronic constipation. A teaspoonful of milk of magnesia will usually bring about results in an ordinary attack of constipation and it can safely be given two or three times, once a day. Any condition not responding to these simple remedies requires treatment by the veterinarian, for dosages of more violent cathartics should not be undertaken by the inexperienced. Doses of even these simple remedies should be cut to one-third or one-half for administration to kittens.

An acid condition in the mother's milk can cause diarrhea in young kittens and the diet of the mother should be adjusted to counteract the acid condition. It is often necessary to remove the kittens from the mother and feed them artificially, for continued feeding of acid milk can cause chronic diarrhea and kill the babies. Doses of bicarbonate of soda (common baking soda) will sometimes relieve the acid condition in the mother, and milk of magnesia tablets, crushed and added to foods, will help too. Feed a strongly liquid diet, with less protein, meat, and fish than usual.

Should the dam be left without her kittens to nurse, her milk must be dried up as quickly as possible to prevent its hardening or caking and causing her considerable distress. Bathe the nipples with a warm solution, half rubbing alcohol, half water, at body temperature several times a day, and cut way down on liquid foods. Give just meat, fish, dry kibble biscuit, dry cereals, or bread crusts to nibble on for several days, or until there are signs that the milk has lessened considerably. Should the milk glands become so filled that the cat is distressed by pressure, take a piece of cloth, dipped in warm water and wrung out, and, wrapping the cloth about your fingers, press the nipples gently to expel the milk and give the cat relief from the discomfort. A cat does not stand pain well, and if she suffers, she will not respond to it well. One cannot give the cat a kitten to nurse, for the kit will suffer if you do. Bandaging the cat rather snugly about the body will aid in reducing the production of milk.

Milk of bismuth is a common and easily administered cure for diarrhea. One-quarter teaspoonful three times a day for not more than two days will usually harden the feces and bring relief from the condition. Once the feces show signs of solidification, becoming just soft rather than liquid in formation, cease the bismuth treatment, for it carries over, coating the intestines for some time.

To treat any infection of the intestinal tract, various sulfa drugs are used. Sulfathiazole, sulfaguanadine, and sulfasuxidine are all efficacious in the treatment of the intestinal tract.

Coccidiosis is a dangerous infection of the intestinal tract and must be treated with sulfa drugs to effect a cure. The bowel movements are liquid yellowish and have a vile odor, most offensive, as in the case of stomach catarrh. Examination of the stool under a microscope by the veterinarian will show whether the condition is coccidiosis or catarrh. Since coccidiosis is very infectious, nursing care is of extreme importance in treating the disease. Dosage is every two hours, the amount and kind to be prescribed by the veterinarian. Administration of medication must be carried out faithfully, with no skipping the time for medicating to make a trip to the store or go on an outing. The cages must be washed with disinfectant each time the cat has a movement of the bowels to prevent re-infection. One must give of time and energy to the nursing of kits or cats with this disease, and it can be cured in jig time if the nurse is faithful and careful. It's no use trying to raise Siamese unless you are prepared to devote much time in case of illness. Any cat which has coccidiosis must be isolated from all other animals to prevent spread of infection.

ROUNDWORMS

The commonest form of worms in cats is the roundworm. This worm is seen in the stool and is sometimes vomited up in food. It is a thin, stringlike worm, about two inches in length, usually curled up in a spiral. The danger from roundworms is that irritation is set up in the stomach and intestines and that the cat does not receive benefit from its food when infested with these parasites. A bad infestation of roundworms shows in the condition of the cat's coat, the fur appearing tacky or separated, never lying really smooth. Another manifestation of these parasites appears in the cat's eyes, the haws being always partly raised across the inner corner of the eye, giving the cat a rather stupid, sleepy look. Bad breath is another symptom of roundworm infestation. Treatment these days is simple, for one needs to give only a pink pill prescribed by the veterinarian, and if the medicine is retained for even a few minutes, and nausea is uncommon from this medication, the dose enters the blood stream, killing the eggs as well as the active parasites. The pill, as it comes to the breeder, is a rather large one, about the size of a five-cent piece, divided into quarters by indented lines. One of these sections is given for each four pounds of weight. It may safely be given to small kits or to pregnant and nursing queens, as I know from experience. There are other good preparations on the market, which can be purchased from supply shops, but this is the one I have used with great success and it must be obtained through the veterinarian by prescription.

TAPEWORMS

Tapeworm is a much more serious infestation than the common roundworm. Segments of the tapeworm are cast off and appear in

Graceful, lithe and lovely, the true beauty of line that is the heritage of the Siamese Cat is epitomized in this photo.

the stools, small white pieces about half an inch long, flat, and seemingly alive with an undulant movement which ceases shortly after exposure to air. The head of the tapeworm is fastened to the small intestine, just below the stomach, and the worm reproduces by division, much as the amoeba multiplies. Worming for tapeworm is useless unless the head is forced loose; indeed, the medicine is rather violent, and unless one is very experienced in all matters relating to animals, it is better to take the cat to the veterinarian and leave him there for worming. Do not feed for at least twelve hours before worming for tapeworm and feed rather lightly afterward for a day.

It is said that tapeworm is conveyed from one animal to another through an intermediary host, usually a flea, and that direct contact with segments cast off by one animal will not affect another. It is, however, to my mind, better to take no chances, and the cat which has tapeworm should be isolated until after he is wormed. Cages used when the animals are wormed should be thoroughly washed with disinfectant when the job is done to prevent re-infection.

A six months old male kitten, Purr-Son of Ebon Mask, bred by V. M. Nelson, and owned by Dr. R. Mosteller, Chattahoochee, Florida.

Tapeworms feed upon the food which the animal host eats, and thus rob the cat of nourishment so that he eventually becomes run-down and weak. It is of utmost importance to be sure, before breeding the queen, that she is free from any infestation of roundworms or tapeworms.

ENTERITIS

This disease, which is commonly known as "infectious enteritis," is infectious panleucopenia, the dread failing of the blood to supply that which is necessary to life. Marked decrease in the white cell count of the blood is always present. Enteritis is a virus which strikes through the intestinal tract, involving in the progress of the illness all of the alimentary canal from mouth to anus. Nothing is more dreaded by the breeder of cats than to have enteritis strike in the home or cattery, and all precautions are taken to avoid contagion.

The ease of transmission is evident when one knows that it can be transmitted even through written correspondence, and that direct contact is not necessary.

First symptom of enteritis is failing appetite, and if the cat's or kitten's temperature is taken at this time, it will read at 102 to 104 degrees, or even higher. Immediate action taken at the onset will bring many kits through enteritis, but action must not be delayed for even a few hours to "see how the kitten is." After the temperature rises it is only a short time until the kit will vomit, a frothy white liquid with traces of yellow bile in it, and as the disease progresses the bile becomes more evident and the frothiness less. The rapidity with which dehydration takes place is almost unbelievable, and injections of saline solution and glucose are needed to keep the kit's body from becoming entirely dehydrated and emaciated. Large doses of homologous serum should be given twice a day, four c.c's per injection, for two days at least, to put into the blood stream the antibodies necessary to fight the virus. Aureomycin is given every four hours, the amount to be prescribed by the veterinarian. This antibiotic works marvels in fighting enteritis virus, while penicillin is useless except to counteract secondary infections which are apt to follow upon the course of enteritis. "Strep throat" is a common secondary infection in enteritis, and penicillin does very well in fighting this, and the not too infrequent pneumonia. These succeeding illnesses are caused by the lowering of the kit's resistance to disease through the weakening of the body by the enteritis, and the lack of white corpuscles in the blood stream to fight invading germs.

The red blood cells are found to be numerous but not healthy in enteritis, and they lack strength to convey oxygen in sufficient quantity to support the kit in its struggle to survive. Fluids must be forced by mouth, and the cat or kit will hang over a water dish, desiring to drink, but unable to swallow because of infection of the throat and a paralysis of the esophagus and muscles used in swallowing.

Pepsin in mild beef broth is good and may be given by dropper, but if the kit does not swallow easily, stroke the throat gently to encourage the action. Easy stroking of the throat encourages an involuntary action of the muscles. In dosing with aureomycin it has been found that the nauseating effects of dosages are counteracted by giving the drug with milk. The combination of streptomycin and penicillin is of great importance, but care must be used, and if the injections are given, they should be administered before the cat becomes weakened by illness, in the earliest stages of the disease. The injection of this combination is apt to produce a sort of shock in the cat, and the animal will have convulsive vomiting and even become unsteady on the legs and appear partially paralyzed within an hour after the injection is given. It is thus an extremely risky method of curing the illness, and should be used only with attendance of the veterinarian.

Nursing is of great importance in attempting to bring kits through a siege of infectious enteritis, and since the mortality rate is so high, one must expect losses. Warmth must be maintained in the effort to keep the temperature to at least normal level, about $101\frac{1}{2}$, until the virus is defeated, for once, the temperature drops below 100 degrees, the battle is lost. Veterinary hospitals are not anxious, generally, to take cases of enteritis for treatment, but prefer that the cat be kept at home and nursed to prevent spread of infection as far as possible. The cat should be confined to a cage, and kept in a draftless place, with an electric heater or hot water bottles to keep him warm. Faithful administration of medicines and feedings are extremely important to keep up the kit's strength. Twenty-four to thirty-six hours will usually tell the story, and the kit will recover and begin to take an interest in life or he will be gone. Post mortem examinations show wide-spread hemorrhage of small blood vessels in the intestinal tract and about the liver and kidneys, with inflammation of the throat and stomach very evident. The body of the cat is greatly dehydrated and emaciated.

Kittens should be given the inoculations for enteritis at three months or earlier, depending upon their size and development. Two injections of the feline anti-distemper vaccine, two cc's per shot, given seven to ten days apart, will give protection. Immunity is not complete until three weeks after the first injection is given. If you suspect that a kit has been exposed to enteritis, injections of the homologous serum, one cc per pound of body weight, should be administered for several days. This puts antibodies into the blood stream at once to fight the infection, but the protection lasts only about ten days. We suggest an injection of the serum for kits which have not been vaccinated, if they are to be shown at the early age of four months. For older cats, a booster shot of vaccine is a good precaution.

Since the passage of the drug act by Congress several years ago, the sulfa drugs—penicillin, aureomycin, and other drugs and vaccines—are not obtainable except with a veterinarian's prescription.

COLDS

The many forms of colds are grouped together and called coryza by most veterinarians. A cold is the ailment which causes the cat to sneeze, have mucus discharge from the nose and throat, and sometimes minor bronchial involvement, with inflammation of the eyes accompanying the other symptoms. Anything more serious or more widespread is pneumonia or a virus infection.

Common coryza is shown when the cat simply sneezes and snorts, but has no symptoms of trouble in throat or chest. Coryza is treated by injections of penicillin to ward off progressive worsening of the trouble, and by forcing fluids, making the cat's diet consist of far more liquid food than he would ordinarily take. Soups, broths, milk, water to which glucose in the form of clear syrup has been added, and injections of a sort of homologous vaccine, are used to treat a genuine common coryza.

Rhinitis follows much the same line of symptoms, but in rhinitis there is apt to be far more serious inflammation and swelling of the eyelids and inflammation of the eye itself. Terramycin has been used with very good results in clearing up rhinitis, with penicillin injections, again, to ward off secondary developments. Terramycin is given in fifty milligram doses, three capsules per day for five days, two each day for three days. Then taper off with one a day for three more days. Some veterinarians recommend heavier doses to begin with, and a shorter term of medicating, but we have found that one is far less apt to have a recurrence or relapse if the dosage is carried out over the longer period of time, and in lesser quantities. Terramycin does not seem objectionable to the cats, and we have mixed it directly into food with no refusal to eat on the part of the animals. Of course, if the cat will not eat, the capsules must be given, but they are very small and administration is not difficult.

Of course, ideally, cats afflicted with colds should be isolated, but, if the cats run the house together, when one has come down, it is almost always too late to do anything to protect the others. However, any sick cat here is caged at once and not allowed to mingle freely with the others. And many times, when some minor infectious illness has struck, some have entirely escaped infection. The big untraviolet lamp comes into play at times when colds are raging, for it does kill airborne germs and sterilizes any surface which is exposed to its rays. Cages should be washed daily with disinfectant. After any siege of illness, cages should be aired out-of-doors and painted before they are used for young cats or new members of the feline family. Cats who have lived together for any length of time develop a certain resistance to diseases, due, we feel, to the fact that they have undoubtedly had minor, sometimes unnoticed, attacks of illnesses which the others have had in more serious form, and an immunity has been set up in them. Newcomers or tiny kittens do not have this immunity and therefore must be protected by every means. Disinfection and painting of quarters are two excellent methods by which to prevent infection of new or young animals who come in contact with cages which have previously been used by older cats.

COLIC: STOMACH UPSETS

Colic is caused, usually, by food that is cold, not near body temperature, when eaten. All foods fed to cats, particularly young cats, should be at room temperature, at least, or warmer. The cat's stomach cannot abide the sudden shock of a mass of cold food, and the stomach contracts, giving the cat pains similar to the pains of gastritis in persons. Formation of gas is caused by the slow digestion of the food which is eaten at too low a temperature, and the cat is apt to suffer from gas pressure in the abdomen and stomach. Colic is recognized by the actions of the cat as well as by his appearance. The cat will drool and become unsteady on his feet, breath will be short and eyes appear glazed. There is no temperature with colic. The abdomen is bloated in appearance, and by palpating it, one can feel the gas roll inside the cat's body. A good two teaspoonfuls of milk of magnesia should be given a grown cat, the dose lessened for younger animals, and the cat kept in a very warm place with hot water bottles or heating pad. If relief does not come soon, an enema should be given, just a small one to promote peristaltic action of the

Champion Cuthpa Alezan, beautiful Chocolate-Point female, bred and owned by Mrs. R. M. Cuthbertson, Lufkin, Texas.

bowel. To give an enema, use a small syringe, an ear syringe will do filled with warm, soapy water, or half warm water and half vegetable oil. Hold the cat by the tail, close to the body, and having previously oiled the tip of the nozzle of the syringe with vaseline, insert it very slightly, and with great gentleness, into the rectum and press the water out of the syringe. Even this small amount of warm water will give the cat a desire to evacuate the bowel, and will start the gas in the intestines moving, relieving the pressure. Colic attacks do not last long, two to three hours at most, and they are over, but the cat looks and is most distressed and his appearance can be quite frightening to the owner. Feed lightly and warmly for a day after an attack of colic.

Ordinary upset stomach is usually due to dietary mistakes, overfeeding, or food of cold temperature, or rapidity in eating. Overfeeding is a common offense of owners against the cat, kindly though it may be meant. Some cats tend to gulp food down without chewing it, and it will be regurgitated almost as soon as it is swallowed when the abused stomach decides it just can't handle such a mass of unmasticated food. With kittens it is sometimes wise to feed all from

Four of a kind, a difficult hand to beat when they are all aces.

one dish, to provide competition and accustom them to eating what is prepared and offered for a meal. No kitten is going to watch his brothers and sisters eat without struggling to get his share of the food. With older cats, separate dishes and places to eat are best, and company often laughs to see me feeding Dru, Petita, and the younger members of the family here in the kitchen. Tita flies to her particular chair, upon which her dish is placed, Dru wants hers on the floor under the chair upon which Tita is dining, and the others divide the rest of the kitchen chairs for dining-tables. One cat had her dish upon a chair, but each bite had to be taken to the floor before it was eaten. If older cats are forced to compete for a share from a communal dish, they will gulp as much as they can swallow in the shortest possible time and will therefore be more apt to have digestive upsets. Meat should ordinarily be chopped rather fine so that, if it is eaten too rapidly, it will not be too much for the stomach to manage; but once in awhile, it is good to feed the cat a large piece of meat he must chew up to eat. This provides exercise for jaws and teeth, as well as forcing the cat to eat slowly, since he must chew off each bit before he can swallow it. If a cat or kit throws up more than one meal, or if there is a sour odor to the vomit, put him on a fast for eighteen hours, giving him nothing but cool, not icy cold, water, and keep him as quiet as possible for this time. A small dose of milk of magnesia will do no harm and will help settle the stomach and increase the flow of gastric juices.

OBSTRUCTIONS

Foreign objects swallowed by small animals can cause a great deal of worry and trouble to the owner as well as pain to the cat or dog. Playthings should be things that the cat cannot chew apart or swallow whole, and all things like pins, needles—especially needles with thread in them—marbles, small rubber bands or garters, sleeve-holders, and jar rings should be kept off the floors or any place where the cat can reach them. Cellophane is a very dangerous plaything, for it does not soften like paper after it is swallowed, but retains its sharp edges which will lacerate the stomach and intestines if it passes through the cat's body. Bleeding results from these lacerations, and if you know that your kit or cat has swallowed anything of this nature, feed soft things like mashed potato and get him to the veterinarian as quickly as possible. Examination under the fluoroscope will show where the obstruction is, its size, and whether it can pass through the intestinal tract or whether surgery will be needed to remove it. A veterinarian we knew some years ago had made a collection of objects removed from the innards of small animals. The collection included golf balls, ping-pong balls, all sorts of rubber balls, rings, pieces of glass and coal, and to top it all off, a nice big needle taken from the throat of a neutered Siamese we owned! I learned then not to leave such things about anywhere the cats could reach them.

ANESTHETICS

Ether is still the most common anesthetic used on animals, but sodium pentothal is taking its place in many operations. Ether has drawbacks due to the fact that respiratory complications quite often arise after its use and the cat must be kept very warm and guarded against drafts for several days after an operation. The pentothal is given intravenously and the cat becomes unconscious almost at once or in a period of a few seconds without the struggle which is usually the accompaniment to administration of ether. During recovery, until consciousness returns, the cat must be turned over frequently, not left lying in one position for long periods of time, to prevent accumulation and settling of fluids in the lungs. Pentothal slows breathing somewhat, and also blood circulation, so the animal needs to be moved a little to aid in correcting this condition. One advantage of the pentothal is the absence of nausea during recovery. Ether is good for small operations such as neutering or tooth removal, but pentothal is easier on the cat for longer operations.

SKIN DISORDERS

Skin troubles are one of the most dreaded afflictions of animals. It is most discouraging to discover spots on the cat where the fur is disappearing and the skin irritated. First thing to do is to take the cat to the veterinarian for diagnosis of the trouble, for there are so many things that can cause these symptoms, and each has its own treatment—guesswork is fatal. Fungus infections are not as much dreaded as in earlier years, for in this field, as in all else, science has developed new and powerful aids. Follow the veterinarian's advice, and do not attempt to prescribe or treat without his help.

Ringworm is a common and persistent infection, and one of the most difficult to clear up. If it is diagnosed immediately, while it is still confined to very small areas, sodium caprylate, twenty percent solution, rubbed well into the spots and surrounding areas until it foams, then left to dry, will cure it; but if it spreads out to wide areas the carpylate is much too irritating to use. Application of tincture of iodine is an old and sometimes quite successful medication, but must be used with discretion so as not to burn the tissues. If the case is far

Medicine Lake Otani, bred and born at Medicine Lake Cattery, owned by Mrs. Adolph Olson, Minneapolis, Minn.

advanced and spread out over the body of the cat, it is almost unbelievably difficult to effect a cure, but your veterinarian can obtain information, in all probability, from the famous Angell Memorial Hospital in Boston of a method used successfully by a doctor there in extreme cases. This involves clipping off the cat's entire coat, and treating the body section by section over a period of three days, and is certainly nothing for an amateur to try.

Skin eruptions due to allergies, which are like eczema, are readily recognized by the trained veterinarian, and the cure of these is avoidance of the offending substance with which the cat is coming into contact or eating. If it is a food, the sources one by one, must be eliminated until the culprit is discovered. Many cats are allergic to milk, fish, or tomato.

Skin disorders may be avoided by keeping the skin healthy and sufficiently lubricated with natural oils. While concentrated fish oils provide maximum vitamin fortification, regular cod-liver oil is best for the kit that is fully independent of his dam and eating a normal diet. One-half teaspoonful of a refined cod-liver oil, as used for small children, given each day, is ample. To prevent excess feeding of vitamin D, codliver oil should be omitted if other preparations containing this vitamin are given.

NEUTERING

The castration of young males can be done any time after they are fully weaned from the mother cat. I have had many kits neutered at ten weeks, with no ill effects, and find that the earlier it is done the less the cat suffers. It is said by many breeders that castration is better done at six months or over, for early neutering tends to make the cat become coarse as he matures, but we have not found it so. Castration does make the cat grow larger than he would have been if left normal, but coarseness depends upon the feeding of the cat. The operation is a simple one, and the more cord that is removed with the testes the better the result of the neutering and the more normal in size the cat appears as he grows. We have not found with Siamese that neutering makes the cats lazy and lethargic, but that they remain lively and active, the only difference being that they are not combative, as are unaltered males.

Spaying of the female cat is a much more serious and complicated operation. The female kit may be spayed any time after she is three months of age, depending upon her size and the strength of the abdominal wall. The incision is so small that usually only one stitch is needed to close it. Many veterinarians prefer to use no bandages after spaying, and I have come to accept this, but the kit or cat must be kept in a small cage for three or four days before she is allowed any freedom, to prevent strain from jumping or running. Freedom should be for short periods the first day and then increased until, at the end of a week after the operation, she is at normal liberty. The custom of not bandaging has the advantage of not marking the cat's coat, and the animal does not suffer any discomfort due to the restrictions of tight bandaging.

We neuter kits sold for pets before they leave Ebon Mask, and have yet (here I cross fingers, and knock on wood though I am not, of course, superstitious) to lose a kitten from operations for castrating or spaying. A veterinarian who is a good surgeon is a blessing to the breeder of cats, and once found, stick to him like glue!

HAIR BALLS

With Siamese, due to their short coats and easy grooming, there is not much danger of the formation of hair balls in the cat's stomach. However, when the cats are shedding heavily, it is wise to take the precaution of giving a teaspoonful of mineral oil once or twice a week to prevent the hair which is swallowed when they groom themselves from forming hard masses or irritating the lining of the stomach.

NERVOUSNESS AND GENERAL DEBILITY

Some Siamese are highly nervous, and these cats need plenty of calcium and vitamin B. Amino consemin is the best form of vitamin B obtainable, we think, and it can be added to broths diluted from meat concentrates, and kittens accept it, as do most older cats, quite readily. Strangely enough, kits and cats who are wool eaters are often cured of this bad habit by dosage of amino consemin. Calcium has the effect of quieting many highly nervous Siamese, especially males. Given in the form of calcium lactate or in a general vitamin and calcium concentrate, it seems to provide something necessary to soothe and settle the highly excitable nervous system of the Siamese. One must, however, use care in administering calcium to males for fear of the formation of deposits in the kidneys, forming stones or gravel. Altogether too many fine males die of kidney gravel, and the subsequent retention of urine and the inflammation of the ureter caused by the gravel. Vitamin A is given to counteract the formation of gravel in males. Urotropine is a common drug used to relieve males or females who suffer from kidney troubles, but it can be obtained only by prescription.

ONYCHECTOMY (DE-CLAWING OF CATS)

As a result of the objections of cat owners to the damage inflicted upon furnishings, other pets, and upon members of the family, a

A proper and comfortable harness and leash for cat-walking.

Inside a Siamese Cattery, showing cages and carriers.

method of removing the claws from the cat's paws has been perfected. The operation is considered minor surgery, but is indeed delicate and must be performed by an experienced veterinarian in order that it be done perfectly, for if it is not done to perfection, the claws will grow again. This operation was reported upon and demonstrated at a Midwest Small Animal meeting, and received acclaim. It is performed under general anesthesia (pentothal or ether) and the cat does not suffer while being operated upon. Many times people resort to putting a healthy cat to sleep, since the cat cannot be restrained from clawing and digging into furnishings, or is difficult to handle. Certainly, if the de-clawing will save the cat's life and make him a more agreeable member of the family, it serves a good purpose.

Personally, I would prefer to keep the claws clipped short, a simple thing to do, or to have done, since it takes only a few minutes. If the cat is hard to manage, the veterinarian should do the clipping, but many cats do not mind it, since it is NOT painful. Good nail clippers can be purchased at any pet supply shop, and the nails should be cut back just to the point where one does not cut into the vein which runs down the heavy part of the claw. I doubt that judges would admit a cat into competition if the claws were removed, for it would be considered a deformity as is any other malformation or scar, but one need hardly consider claws in the show cat. They are a part of the entire animal, and must be kept. Most scratching of upholstered furniture is done to trim the cat's claws, and remove the out-growing shells from the claws. If the claws are clipped, the cat does not NEED to scratch, and the sharp points are removed without any effort on his part.

CANCER

Cancer occurs about as frequently in animals as it does in people, and the animal system reacts in about the same way. If at any time you discover a lump or hard spot on the cat's body be sure to have an immediate examination made by the veterinarian. Cancer occurs most frequently in females in the breasts and generative organs. Early care is imperative, for if the condition is discovered early enough, removal of the lump may be complete before metastasis has occurred. If the tumor is malignant rather than benign, early excision is of the utmost importance, for the great fatality of animal life in cancer is due to the fact that metastasis happens early in the progress and growth of the malignancy. Metastasis means that cells of the original cancerous growth are freed into the bloodstream and are carried to other parts of the body to start new growths in other organs.

If a queen develops a malignancy, she should not be bred again, but should be spayed. Breeding will only hasten the end and the kittens will not be good, healthy ones, for the queen's own body is striving to throw off the invading growth and weakening her. Once the queen, or any cat for that matter, begins to show signs of distress and pain it is by far the more merciful course to have her gently put to sleep. Sometimes cancer progresses in such a way that there is no pain, just a gradual failing and weakening of the cat's abilities and in this case one can, without cruelty, allow the illness to take its natural course. It is a decision which each of us must make according to our consciences and convictions.

ANTIBIOTICS EFFECTIVE IN CATS

Penicillin is useful for treatment of abscesses and inflammatory exudates.

Erythormycin is used for general infections.

Streptomycin is of aid in combatting enteric and urinary infections.

Terramycin is useful for pulmonary and rhinitis infections. Rhinitis is very stubborn but responds quite remarkably to dosage with terramycin.

Tetracycline for general infections and enteritis infections.

Bactiracin occasionally effective for dysentery.

Neomycin occasionally effective in urinary infections.

ANABOLICS

Anabolics—"old-age pills"—are new in general use. With old age, and sometimes even with middle age, the general health of cats fails. The balanced blend of hormones, as provided by these "pills," should aid in improving their general well-being, especially their coat, temperament, etc., thus adding years to their life-span. While heretofore anabolics have been given mainly to dogs, they should also benefit felines.

EUTHANASIA

Euthanasia is a subject upon which there are very divided feelings among animal lovers. My own personal feeling is that it is kinder to an animal to put him painlessly to sleep than to allow him to suffer from a known incurable illness or injury. It takes courage to do this, make no mistake about it, for in all of us there is the feeling that the taking of life is wrong, and one must gather all his resolution to put a loved pet to sleep, but I have had it done and would again under like circumstances. It seemed the greatest and the last kindness I could do for a cat who was dearly loved by us all and who would have suffered greatly if I had not put it to sleep. When the time comes that a cat is in unremitting pain or is so debilitated that life is a burden rather than a joy, then one must make up his mind and heart as to whether he should or can see his pet go painlessly to sleep never to wake again.

Veterinarians find it rather difficult to suggest euthanasia to people even when they know that there is no hope for recovery or return to good health for an animal, knowing as they do that people are attached to a pet. Try to think of your cat first and your own sentiments last and accept the fact that it is a far greater kindness to put your pet to sleep than to see him in pain which cannot be eased.

This chapter has not been written to bring to your mind all the terrible possibilities of sickness that the cats can suffer, but to provide you with some slight knowledge of how to recognize illness and how to care for the cats when illness does strike. Make full use of your veterinarian's service, for your cat has no better friend.

A top winning champion, this fine Seal-Point Siamese show cat is the proud property of Mrs. Julia Kohlus, of East Rockaway, Long Island. Mrs. Kohlus is a member of the Empire Cat Club.

CHAPTER 8

THE STANDARD
OF JUDGING THE SIAMESE

THE standard for judging Siamese is plain and easily understood if one has knowledge of and feeling for the cats. We will here consider the standard, step by step, and explain it to the best of our ability. Deep knowledge of the cats and that subtle feeling for what is right or wrong in their conformation are not won overnight. It takes years of experience and observation to train the eye to judge Siamese properly. More than the eye is concerned in judging, for the sense of touch, feeling the texture of the coat and the balance of the cat's construction are used. Handling also is necessary.

The shows of the present reach tremendous proportions, an average all-breed show having two hundred or more entries. Of late years an entry of seventy-five to a hundred Siamese is not unusual, and in some west-coast shows the numbers run even higher. Choosing the best cats from among so many fine specimens is not an easy task, and not one for a timid or unknowing soul.

The standard used by the largest of the American organizations sponsoring shows, and followed closely, but with minor variations by the other sponsoring groups, is as follows:

BODY COLOR: 15 POINTS

Body color to be even pale fawn or cream, shading gradually into lighter color on stomach and chest. The coat should not be gray. Body color in older cats allows for deeper color, but there should be definite contrast between body color and points. Proper color: four points. Proper shading: four. Evenness of color: seven points.

Here we come to differing opinions as to interpretation of cream and fawn. Cream can run from an off-white to a deep ivory tone and is very lovely, provided the contrast between body color and points is not lost due to pale pigmentation. Fawn is a color impossible to describe in words, for the color is that of the animal of the same name, the young deer, a reddish light brown which deepens with maturity but still retains its warmth of tone. A paler shade of this color is preferred in the Siamese, and cats are penalized for having too much depth of body color. People sometimes mistake beige for fawn, and this is distinctly wrong, for beige is an artificial color, not seen in nature. Fawn is more reddish in its brown tone than is beige.

COLOR VS. TYPE

Too much emphasis is put upon variables like "belly-spots" in the Siamese. The dark spot on the belly or abdomen is a changeable facet of pigmentation, sometimes light, sometimes dark, and at times not evident at all. A dark streak is often seen on the abdomen of nursing queens, due to the fact that they have recently nursed kittens. It is the height of folly to penalize a fine cat for this, for we would not wish our top stock NOT to breed. The Fancy would regress rather than progress if this happened. One sees judges who look for minor faults like the belly-spot, and often a fine cat is put down for little reason other than the temporary existence of this fault. To the competent judge, type is of first consideration, and color is considered secondly. The cat must be considered as a whole, not just as an accumulation of items, but rather as an entity, everything combined to make a harmonious whole, a cat of superior quality who is a boon to the Fancy.

Young Siamese have paler coats—says the standard—but here again we see differences of opinion. Some breedings produce kits of rather smutty and dark coloring, and by the time these babes are five to six months old one can see, just by turning back the coat hairs, a paler color coming up from the skin. Even in the truly pale-coated kitten one does not desire a "white" coat, for no matter how pale the color it should be warm in tone. Grayness is distinctly undesirable, as stated in the standard. It is true that Siamese darken somewhat with age and that we admire a pale coat, BUT the dark coat unless it is so intense as to eliminate contrast between coat and points is not to be deplored. As long as the coat retains evenness and warmth of color along with sufficient contrast to the points, it is not too serious if the cat carries a fairly dark coat.

POINTS: 10 POINTS

Mask, ears, legs and tail, dense and clearly defined, all of the same shade of deep seal-brown. Mask should be connected with the ears

Champion Oriental Nanki Poo of Newton has champion offspring throughout the country.

When in full coat, like these two lovely Siamese, the frequently used descriptive term for the Siamese coat, "chiffon velvet," is completely apt. The clear blue, almond-shaped eyes are frequently crossed, a characteristic exhibited by the cat at the right, but through a knowledge of cat genetics, coupled with rigid selection, this latter trait is being controlled and gradually eliminated from the breed.

by tracings, except in kittens. Mask: two. Ears: two. Legs: two. Feet: two. Tail: two.

The points should end definitely, the mask being clear-cut in shape, not running down into the throat or darkening the top of the head and the spots before the ears. This darkening of color on the head is termed a "hood," the entire head of the cat seemingly of a solid dark color, lacking the paler color in front of the ears, on top of the head, and on lower sides of cheeks. The points should be even without ticking or pale hairs appearing, or rings on tail, or bars on haunches and tops of legs. The chin of the Siamese should be dark, continuing the color of the mask below the mouth. Pale chins are a fault in pigmentation, and in viewing the cat head-on, one should see the chin as dark, NOT paler than the upper lips and face. Personally, I feel that not enough emphasis is put upon good point color by many judges. Pale coats are admired and seem to influence many judges to "set up" a cat, even though the cat may be very lacking in point development. A balance between body and point color should exist, showing the beautiful contrast which forms one of the real facets of beauty in the Siamese.

Mrs. Duncan Hindley, breeder and owner of the world famous Prestwick Siamese Cats, seen here critically judging a kitten for export.

Mrs. Charles L. Jones holding Lamar's Satyra after winning Best Cat In Show at the Southern California Short Hair Breeders second annual show in 1949.

SHAPE OR TYPE OF BODY: 20 POINTS

Body should be medium in size, dainty, long and svelte. Neck, long and slender. Legs, proportionately slim: hind legs slightly higher than the front. Feet, small and oval in shape. Tail, long and tapering with no visible kinks. Body: seven. Neck: four. Legs and Feet: five. Tail: four.

The body of the Siamese is long and rangy, giving a lithe and svelte appearance to the cat. There should be no evidence of fat, and the muscles should appear as the cat moves, high-lighting the haunches and shoulders of the cat when the animal is moving. The belly should be firm, not loose or bulgy, and should hollow-up under the abdomen, somewhat like that of a Greyhound, but not to such an extreme extent. The upward tilt given the body by the long hind legs emphasizes this effect. In proper conformation the body should not, at any point, be wider than the rib cage, nor should the rib cage be much wider than the shoulders, viewed from above.

The question of size in the Siamese can become quite a controversial one, but the standard calls for a medium-sized animal, not larger than the ordinary domestic short-haired cat. The breeders

109

seem to prefer them a trifle smaller, if anything, and in this I concur. But, in this, as in so many things, there are exceptions. What strikes one viewer as large may seem quite average to another, and what strikes one as being very small, may appear just dainty and neat to another. We run up against that old word "proportion" again in considering size in Siamese. There is no good or valid reason for penalizing a good cat, one finely typed and balanced, because of size; for if the proportions are really fine, the size, unless the cat be gigantic or dwarfed, matters little. I remember well a Siamese male of some years past whom I admired tremendously, considering him one of the best I had seen over the years. He was a truly large cat, but because of his grand type and beautifully balanced body, one was not conscious of size, only of beauty. Then, again, some of the cats I have admired most have been tiny cats, dainty almost to the point of fragility in appearance, though all were strong, healthy breeders. Our own Ch. H.R.H. of Ebon Mask seldom weighs over six pounds, but he is "all cat," an active, muscular, well-proportioned male, so that he does not appear delicate and tiny. If large size leads to an appearance of coarseness, then it is to be deplored and will be penalized in judging.

Foreleg and Paw showing the slenderness of the limb and the oval foot.

A Siamese should always appear fine-boned and racy, never heavy.

The legs of the Siamese are long and slim, but well-turned and shapely, not stick-like. One does not admire shapelessness in the legs of the Siamese any more than in people. The cat's legs should be muscular and slender in proportion to the general build of the cat. Feet should be small and oval, the second toe longer than the rest, giving an oval shape to the paw. Hind legs are longer than front legs, so that the cat when standing has a slight upward slant from shoulder to rump.

The Siamese has a long neck, separating the head very definitely from the shoulders. In adult males the neck sometimes thickens, but this, like the jowls, is usually due to holding, and if the cat is otherwise streamlined in type, one makes allowance for this superficial thickening of jowl and neck in an active stud cat. We have found that if a male is withheld from stud until he is past eighteen months he will develop far less jowliness and less thickening of the neck, regardless of how active a stud he may be after he is nearing two years of age. Males allowed to sire before they are a year almost inevitably develop very heavy, thick necks.

The tail of the Siamese should be long, but there is a limit to length as well as to shortness of tail. The ideal provides that the tail measure in length the same distance as from base of tail, where it leaves the body, to a spot between the shoulders, touching the base of the back of the neck. Proportion here as elsewhere in the cat is of importance. If one really knows his Siamese, he can close his eyes and run his hand from the cat's nose, over the head, neck and body, and up to the tip of tail, and his hand will stop where the tail should end. The tail should taper; in other words, the vertebrae are graduated in size from base of the spine to tip of tail, the end piece being pointed. The kink in the Siamese tail is a genetic inheritance and has not been successfully bred out of the cats despite sincere efforts. It is often seen even today here and in England in cats of the finest breeding, really top show-winners, cats of top breeding and wonderful specimens of their breed. The kink is not of great importance as long as it is not noticeable, but must be felt, and as long as it involves only the last or next-to-last vertebrae. Malformation of the tail higher up, bobbed, hooked, or double-kinked tails are grounds for disqualification in the judging ring. In fact, any kink that shows to the naked eye is grounds for withholding championship status from a

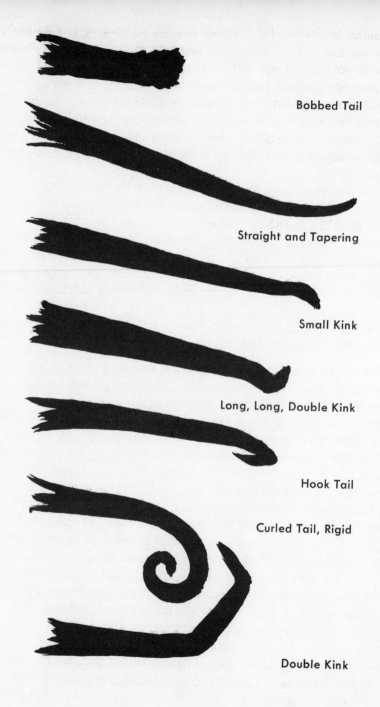

Bobbed Tail

Straight and Tapering

Small Kink

Long, Long, Double Kink

Hook Tail

Curled Tail, Rigid

Double Kink

Siamese. Pet owners like the kink in many cases, for it is definitely a Siamese trait; but we who try to breed for showing purposes do not like to see it crop up, and it does, make no mistake about that. Mating two cats with perfectly straight tails does not insure straight-tailed kittens; that I have learned by experience; and sometimes mating two cats who both have doubtful tails, slightly kinked, or not quite long enough, will turn out litter after litter of kittens with long, tapered tails, conforming to the requirements of the standard to a "tail."

HEAD AND EARS: 20 POINTS

Heads should be long and should taper in straight lines from the ears to a narrow muzzle, with no break at the whiskers. The receding chin caused by the failure of the upper and lower teeth to meet in a straight line shall be considered a serious fault. The skull shall be flat, and the nose is to be a continuation of the forehead with no break. In profile, a straight line is to be seen from the center of the forehead to the tip of the nose. Allowance to be made for jowls in the stud cat. There should be the width of an eye between the eyes. Ears rather large and pricked, wide at base. Long Flat Profile: six. Fine muzzle: four, Non-Receding Chin: four. Width between Eyes: two. Ears: four.

I find the terminology "width between the eyes" rather misleading, and breeders who have handled the cats for many years know that the entire head is wedge-shaped, not just from the eyes to the muzzle. In fact the width should be greatest at the point where the ears are placed on the skull. Too many cats whose heads narrow into straight sides above the eyes are being shown lately. The shape of the skull is something like an egg, oval, the narrow end at the nose when viewed from on top. The length of the head is approximately one and one-third the width at the widest point where the ears are set. There must be no sudden narrowing in or pinching of the bone just below the eyes, for this formation results in a muzzle which does not taper to a fine end but is apt to be square or chopped off in appearance. Sometimes a cat will habitually, when nervous, throw the whiskers forward giving a false impression of broadness at the whisker pads, but it can be discerned by touch whether the muzzle is truly square or tapered. Despite the phrase "straight lines" in describing

Ear placement of the Siamese in accordance with the official standard.

the face of the Siamese in the standard, one must realize that in nature there is no such thing as a straight line, for nature abhors the straight line as she does the vacuum, and even apparently straight lines are gently curved. The Siamese head is a series of gently blended lines, harmonious and beautiful.

In profile, too, the head is a wedge, but with the narrow, or nose end cut off abruptly, forming a nice, firm muzzle in which the chin is in line with the nose. An expression used to describe the head of the Siamese is "snaky" and it is apt, to say the least. The profile wedge is deepest at the point where the ears are set, just above the jaw-hinge. From the center of the forehead, above the eyes, the profile should be straight to the end of the nose, unbroken by any dip between the eyes. By running the finger from the tip of the nose to the forehead one can feel whether the bone bends or whether any observable break is just a rising of the fur at this point. The back of the skull should show behind the ears, not fall straight down to the neck from the ears.

The ears must be large and wide open at the base, with very little hair showing in them. The ears taper to almost pointed tips. In England, and under the judges of America's largest registering body, ears which flare slightly outward are preferred to erect ears. This minor outward turn to the ears gives the effect of continuing the wedge-shape of the face to the very top of the head, and is attractive, but the ears must not flare so far out as to appear donkeyish. A pricked ear is one which slants slightly forward, giving an impression of alertness and attention, as if the cat were attracted by some sound or sight. It is true that the ears must be large, but they should not be so long or heavy in size as to overbalance the delicate construction of the head.

EYES: 20 POINTS

Eyes shall be clear and of a vivid deep-blue color. Eye aperture almond in shape and slanting towards the nose in true oriental fashion. Color: ten. Clear: five. Deep blue: five. Shape. ten. Oriental: five. Uncrossed: five.

The eye of the Siamese is one of the most attractive features of this altogether fascinating animal. It is entirely unlike the eye of any other feline—except those related to the Siamese through crossbreeding or origin. The shape is described as almond and that is an approximately correct description, but the eye is somewhat wider than the almond, though never round. The upper lid must cut across the inner corner of the eye to give the proper tilted shape, and the outer corner of the eye should be much higher than the inner corner. The eye need not be small to appear properly shaped, for a large eye can still be slanted and narrow and is very attractive.

In color the eye is to be, according to the standard, a deep blue— and the expert describes it as "Sapphire Blue," meaning the oriental

Correct Siamese Cat's eye.

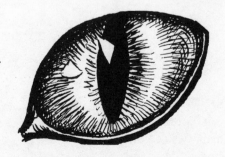

sapphire of that beautiful depth of color. The eye must be deep in color but never dull, rather of a great brilliance almost as if a light were behind the eye. Inbreeding sometimes produces a deep blue eye but the depth of eye color produced by this method is dull, lacking brilliance. The true oriental sapphire is a dark blue, almost navy, but always with glitter and reflected light in its depths. This eye color is one of the attractive aspects about our Siamese and is unlike that of any other creature, for the other animals having blue eyes do not have a deep blue eye, rather a pale sky blue. It almost always surprises the novice on his first sight of a Siamese in the flesh to see the blue eye in the midst of the almost black face, and in most cases seals the interest of the novice fast.

COATS: 10 POINTS

Short, fine in texture, glossy and lying close to the body. Short Coat: three. Fine Coat: two. Glossy Coat: two. Close Coat: three.

Sky Lolo Panther la Quinn, Blue-Point Siamese show winner, owned by Mrs. Elsie Quinn, El Monte, California.

Mrs. Beaver's beautiful, trophy-winning, Seal-Point Champion.

This description of the Siamese coat leaves very little for illustration. The coat shall be short, period. It is to cling closely to the skin, and be glossy and fine. A too heavy coat may have an attractive velvety appearance but it is not what the standard requires, and a rather long coat may cling closely, but again, this does not conform to requirements. Shortness and sleekness combined produce that appearance of satiny slinkiness in the cat, the coat shining with highlight with every movement of the body.

CONDITION: 5 POINTS

Good physical condition. Not fat; inclined to muscle.

If the cat is in good condition, he looks it. The muscles are hard, and the cat is slender with no layer of fat distributed over the body to hide the fundamental type of the cat. Exhibitors sometimes feel that a judge penalizes too heavily for condition or rather, lack of it, when scoring a cat, but what these people do not realize is that lack of condition affects all of the cat, hiding the fundamental construction and boning under a layer of blubber, making the cat appear heavy all over. Hence, the cat may lose on "legs," "feet," "tail," "neck," etc. So in order to do your cat justice, do not enter him in a show if he is noticeably overweight, rather hold him back and slim him down for a succeeding show. It is not fair to show a cat at a disadvantage when he may be good enough to make a high win when he is in good condition. It is said by some breeders that a cat should be allowed to eat all he wants, and that type is not true unless it appears despite this overfeeding. We know that many human beings have to diet for the sake of health and appearance, and are still well fed and not hungry. It is no kindness to allow your Siamese to be overweight, for it puts a strain upon the heart and other vital organs. Neither should he be so thin as to feel bony. A good layer of solid muscle should pad the bones and make him feel hard and muscular when handled, not soft and flabby or bony.

In outlining the standard and its explanations, I have used the standard for Seal-Pointed Siamese, since they are the dominant color. But this same standard applies to all other Siamese with the exception of the points given for color.

The Blue-Pointed Siamese has a body of a glacial white, very pale with a faint bluish cast to it, any darker shading being of the same tone as the points. The points are a gray-blue, providing definite contrast with the body color. Eyes a clear and bright china blue rather than the deep blue of the Seal-Point's eyes.

The proper judging of eye color has been discussed, but this standard, used by the principal governing organizations, is specific in that it requires different shades of eye color for all accepted varieties of Siamese: deep sapphire-blue for the Seals, brilliant china blue for the Blue Pointed and Chocolates, and a light, even blue for the Frosts.

This would be the correct color also for the Red-Points, which, however, are not yet recognized by the largest organization. The Red-Point is included in the Siamese classification by majority vote of the members of the Siamese Section of the American Cat Fanciers' Association.

The Chocolate-Pointed Siamese has a coat of a pale ivory tone with no appreciable shading, a clear color all over, and the points are of a deep milk-chocolate shade. The nose leather and foot pads are a pinkish brown, rather like the chocolate tone of the points but with

Mrs. Girard D. Kelsey, Siamese judge of Pennsylvania, with a Best-In-Show Siamese winner, the Seal-Point, Chindwin's Tana of Wu. This lovely female Siamese was bred by Everett Battey and owned by Lillian King of Revere, Mass.

the reddish tone from the blood showing through. Eyes a china blue, much like those of the Blue-Pointed Siamese, but may be somewhat darker with propriety.

In Chocolate-Pointed kittens the nose and paws remain almost a true pink for some weeks; then the nose shows the faint brownish tinge, but the pads take much longer to develop the chocolate coloring. Chocolate-Pointed kittens have an almost dead-white coat, paler than that of the palest Seal-Pointed kittens who, no matter how pale, have a warm tinge to the body color. In Seal-Pointed kits the skin of the edges turns back within days of birth, but the Chocolate kitten has skin on the ears which is a soft, not dark, brown at eight weeks

Ch. Pagan of the Dark Guantlets, Seal-Point male, who made his championship although not shown until he was nine years old. Breeder, Mrs. R. P. Hokin; owners, Mr. and Mrs. Leigh Manley, Arcata, California.

or more. The Chocolate-Pointed cat has come into high favor in the past eight years and is increasing in numbers at a rapid rate. They are truly lovely when they are good, soft and delicate in coloring, but the poor ones look like faded Seal-Points and are not attractive.

The Frost-Pointed Siamese is to the Blue-Point as the Chocolate is to the Seal. Body color of an even glacial white without shading, and points frosty gray with a very faint pinkish tone. The Frost-Point is expected to be quite a dainty cat, a little smaller in size than the Seal- or Blue-Point, and is not considered to be entirely matured in development and size until between two and three years of age. The nose pad is of a faded lilac tint and the paw pads are a salmon pink. Eyes to be a clear china blue, bright and colorful.

The Frost-Pointed Siamese are being raised in considerable numbers in America, but are most numerous on the West Coast, not very many appearing at shows in the Eastern section.

A Siamese of a color for which there is no standard, but one of the most attractive cats I have ever seen, is the one with almost purplish points, much darker than a Blue-Point, nose and pads a deep lavender shade, and very dark blue eyes of wonderful brilliance. Apparently the one I have seen is an oddity, and there are no others of like coloring, for kittens have not been shown with this coloration. The pedigree background of this male contained Blue- and Seal-Point, and apparently a Chocolate factor for breeding, also. The Blue-Point in the pedigree was back four or more generations from the Lavender cat. I rather wish some breeders who have large numbers of cats with suitable accommodations would do some definite breeding to try to fix this coloring and type, for they are very beautiful.

JUDGING THE SIAMESE

Judging is not easy, for there are so many fine cats in America today that choosing a winner from among them is no task for the novice or for one who does not know Siamese through long years of breeding and study. More Siamese breeder-judges are needed, and it is encouraging to see new names on the lists of judges. Mistakes are made, of course, as in any human endeavor, but the young judges will learn and the improvement of the Siamese as a breed depends largely upon the right cats winning at the shows. It is not enough to be satisfied with one's personal gains through taking rosettes and ribbons at a show. One must develop an impartial attitude and wish to see the best cat win, even if one's own cat suffers defeat as a result. The shows are not held as social or sporting events, but are run to bring out the better cats so that breeders may see how the Siamese are improving and to help them plan for improving their own stock to meet the high standards set by the winners. The cat fancy has grown to such an extent that the breeding of cats is no longer just the hobby of a few people, but has developed into a business involving much money. Since the purebred Siamese comprise half or more of all registrations made here and in England each year, they deserve the best available judging, and only years of breeding and experience in handling will make outstanding judges with the knowledge of what is right and proper in Siamese.

A judge cannot, justifiably, set up a cat because he is partial to some one quality in Siamese and this cat has "it." He must evaluate all facets of the cat, scoring each animal individually against the standard as it is set down for guidance. Should he have in competition two animals of like score, he must then judge them, one against

Champion Amdos Yan-Kee, Seal-Point male. Bred by Mme. A. M. D'Ollone. Owned by Mr. and Mrs. S. S. Nelson.

Champion Kay Bee Mia Lescula, an imported, Blue-Point female. Breeder; Mrs. Kennedy-Bell, England. Owner; Mrs. Alexander Pinney.

the other, taking age and development into consideration in order to choose a winner between them. A dark body tone may be counter-balanced by terrific point color, or, conversely, rather pale points be balanced by a pale, clear body which is very lovely.

Of course, these are my personal views and convictions. Though I have shown numerous cats in almost twenty years of breeding Siamese, garnering my share of bests, I hope to see not only more Siamese breeder-judges at the shows, but also better-quality cats. Now that one organization requires a prospective judge to have bred cats in his chosen classification for at least five years, more equable and generally improved show results should be the rule. If there were no clubs to stage shows, there would be no Fancy to benefit breeders and cats.

A lovely headstudy of the Blue-Point female, Grand Champion Dark Guantlets Desmine. Owner, Mrs. Fredric Hokin, of Arcadia, California. The breeders of Desmine are, Mr. and Mrs. Leigh Manley.

CHAPTER 9

ORGANIZATIONS OF THE CAT FANCY

IN the United States at the present time there are five organizations for the registration of purebred cats and for sponsoring shows. These organizations have clubs in every state in the Union and in most of the large cities of the nation.

The oldest of the five organizations is the American Cat Association with headquarters in Chicago, and its member clubs are spread from coast to coast. The American Cat Fanciers' Association is the newest of the five and has headquarters in Texas, but its membership, held individually, is spread over the entire country. The idea of individual voting memberships is a new one in the Fancy, and ACFA is the first organization to offer them to its members. This association is inaugurating many new features in its show rules, including a school for judges, held usually in conjunction with some large show. The largest organization is the Cat Fanciers' Association, Inc., which is nationwide and composed of nearly 100 clubs. The Cat Fanciers' Federation and the United Cat Federation are the other two organizations. All of the clubs maintain registration books in which cattery names and the pedigrees and names of individual cats are permanently registered.

Show rules of the organizations are fairly similar, those of the ACFA showing greater deviation from the others, since they are inaugurating many procedures not commonly used heretofore.

WHAT THESE ASSOCIATIONS ARE

The member clubs are formed by groups of people interested in cats, regardless of kind, to promote interest in and knowledge of cats among the general public, to promote the welfare of cats and to provide a common meeting ground for the interests of the members. The clubs usually have some social affairs each year, such as, dinners, picnics and teas, but the principal aim of the clubs is not social but definitely devoted to the betterment of the cats with interest centered, naturally, upon the purebred, pedigreed stock which the members maintain and show.

The clubs have their individual constitutions, governing the running of shows, committees, etc., but these constitutions must meet the approval of the parent organization's board of directors before they become official. Amendments in these club constitutions must be approved by the parent organization before they may be added to the club's own rules. Shows are run under the show rules and regulations of the organization to which the club belongs. Arrangements for shows follow a more or less set pattern, beginning with the request for permission to run the show, which must be granted by the board of directors, who must approve also the choice of judges. The various orgnaizations issue a list of approved or novice judges from which the clubs may select judges for all-breed shows, and for the various specialty shows held in conjunction with an all-breed

Grand Champion Kewalo Lei Krampert, Blue-Point male, bred by Miss P. F. Alexander, and owned by Mr. and Mrs. E. W. Krampert of Casper, Wyoming. This was the first Siamese male grand champion in the United States.

show. Some judges are limited to a specific breed such as Siamese; others may be accredited to do all Short-Hairs, still others qualified only for Persians, etc. Specialty shows are sponsored by clubs which specialize in the particular breed or classification of feline to be shown, and rosettes and ribbons are offered by these clubs to exhibitors in the specialty shows. Only specialty clubs may run a show without an accompanying all-breed show, and in California there is a Short-Hair show each year. Siamese Specialty Clubs are numerous, and there is a solid color Specialty Club for each section of the country. All the clubs and the organizations advertise in **Cats Magazine,** and information can be obtained simply by writing to the secretary of any club in which one may be interested.

CAT SHOWS

A club does better financially if it runs two or three specialties together with an all-breed show, for the greatest expense of the show is, after renting a suitable hall, the expense of hiring or owning cages. The specialty shows bring in double entry fees and encourage a larger entry, for people who must travel some distance to show their cats will do so more readily if the advantage of an opportunity to show under two judges, rather than one, and the chance of gaining extra points towards a championship are offered.

Prize money and awards are solicited from members of other clubs and from the fancy as well as cup lists of other clubs upon which exhibitors may make wins. Advertising in the catalog helps defray the cost of the show, and both breeders and manufacturers of products used by the fancy will take ads in show catalogs to support the show. Gifts of cash are made to the show funds, and veterinarians give their services to the shows gratis.

All cats are examined by a veterinarian before entering the show room, and any sign of skin disease, ear troubles, runny eyes or sniffles, in fact, anything which might be infectious and endanger the other exhibits will bar a cat from the show room. Cats may not be benched until they have passed the veterinarian's inspection and have a card signed by him to put on the cage, signifying that the animal was in good health when it entered the show room. If any animal shows signs of illness during a show, it will be examined by the doctor who decides whether the cat is ill or just nervous and homesick, and if he decides that the animal is really ill, it is immediately removed from the show room. This is for the protection of other cats entered in the show.

Shows usually run for two days, but there is no rule against one- or three-day shows. Due to the large entries in recent times, specialties are judged throughout the show. Kitten classes are judged first, followed by novices, open classes, champions and grand champions, and neuters. The number of championship points awarded at a show depends upon the size of the entry, the number of cats entered in the show, the winner of the novice class competing against the winner in the open class, in each color and sex division, for the "Winners" points and ribbon. It is not possible for a cat to make a championship at one show usually, though under the rules of one organization there may be five specialties in conjunction with the all-breed show, providing opportunity for a cat to make sufficient wins under three different judges to accumulate the necessary points for a championship. Since wins under three judges are required for issuance of a championship certificate in the other organizations, and a cat may be shown only in the all-breed and one specialty show, it follows that cats must attend more than one show to attain championship status. Grand Champions are cats which have won "Best Champion" under three judges of all-breed or specialty shows; one point is awarded for each three champions competing. There are quite a few Grand Champion Siamese, both Seal- and Blue-Pointed, in the United States now.

The organizations hold annual meetings, usually during winter months or in the spring, at which delegates from the member clubs elect officers and directors for the organization for the following year. Only ACFA deviates from this practice, all its officers and directors being elected by the entire membership of the organization. In the other organizations, delegates come to this meeting with instructions from their own clubs on how to vote according to the wishes of the members of the club, and in case of lack of instruction they are to vote for the best interests of the clubs and the fancy as a whole.

Action upon matters of importance to the clubs is taken at the annual meetings, but minor affairs are usually deferred to the board meeting of the directors following the annual meeting and election of officers.

All in all, the fancy is well organized, and every possible opportunity provided to help the clubs and to bring knowledge of the cats and the fancy to the public. People wishing to join member clubs may

Champion Doneraile Drusilla, an imported Seal-Point Siamese female, bred by Mrs. K. R. Williams, and owned by Mr. and Mrs. S. S. Nelson.

contact the secretary of any member club and receive information and application blanks. All the organizations and many of the member clubs run advertisements in **Cats Magazine,** and names and addresses of the secretaries are given in these ads.

Proceeds from the shows are usually presented to some worthy cause, an animal rescue league, a home for crippled children, the March of Dimes, the Red Cross, the Cerebral Palsy Fund, or some other charity which deserves support. Most clubs retain only enough to enable them to do pre-show printing and advertising for the next year's show. The monies given to various charities each year represent a sizeable sum, so the cats help others while bringing entertainment to the public and consolidating the interests of the breeders.

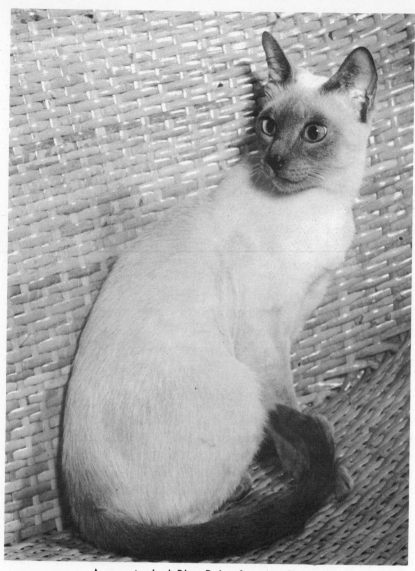

A very typical Blue-Point female, Champion Rockdene's Kannika. The breder-owner of this excellent Siamese is Mrs. John R. Pruett, of Swarthmore, Pennsylvania.

CHAPTER 10

SHOWING AND GROOMING YOUR SIAMESE

SINCE competition in today's shows is so keen, everything must be done to present an animal in the best possible condition so that he may compete on even terms with other fine cats. Grooming is of extreme importance, and there is much that can be done to bring a cat to the pink of perfection. Judges do not, I think, penalize heavily enough cats brought into the showroom in poorly groomed condition. It is neglectful to the cat and rather insulting to the judge for an exhibitor to present before the judge a cat whose coat has not been brushed free of dead hair, or a cat which is not clean.

Siamese, more than any other breed, reflect in their appearance the general condition. Sickness will bring light hairs into the mask and tail, and lighten the front paws. The points must be clear in color, unticked with light hairs, at show time, and it is better to skip a show than to present a cat which is in off-condition.

GROOMING YOUR SIAMESE

Grooming is not a job to be done the last two weeks before a show, but must be faithfully performed during the entire year to keep a cat in top condition. The coat sheds heavily during the spring and summer, and the dead hair must be removed each day to keep it from affecting the new coat as it comes in. Dead hairs remaining in the points will appear lighter than the rest of the point color, and show up as ticking. The best method we have found for removing the dead hair is to brush and massage with a round rubber scalp massager which fits the palm of the hand and has flexible, rounded teeth over its entire surface. Even from a cat which does not seem to be shedding out heavily, much dead hair will come out in the massager. Do not neglect the legs and tail, but brush them just as you do the rest of the body. Follow the brushing with a combing with a very fine-toothed flea comb, being gentle so as not to scratch the skin. Fleas can cause so many troubles that one should do everything possible to keep the cat free of them. Most flea powders contain

DDT, to which cats are allergic, and these powders, unless the DDT is in very small percentage, are unsafe for use with cats. Shampoos which show noticeable amounts of DDT should also be avoided.

BATHING, CLEANING, BRUSHING

If you decide to shampoo your cat—and, please, do not wash a Siamese for at least a week or more before a show, for it will give the coat a fluffy appearance—prepare everything for the bath before you catch the cat. Have two basins of warm water ready, brush and cloth for washing, towels on hand, and then place the cat gently in one basin of water, being careful not to splash the water about. It is the noise and strangeness which frighten the cat more than the water, to which, if it is of body temperature, the cat does not object strenuously. Dampen the coat thoroughly, holding the cat by the scruff of

Brushing brings life and glow to your cat's coat, it invigorates the skin and helps keep both hair and skin clean.

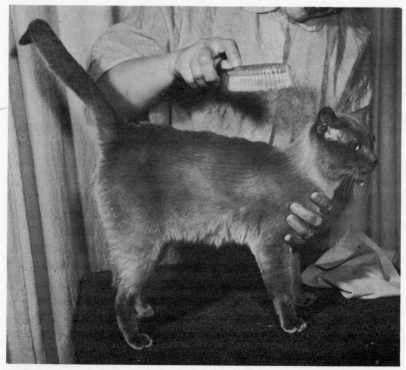

the neck with one hand, or, if you have someone to help you, have him hold the cat, leaving your two hands free to get the shampoo over with that much more quickly. A few drops of the shampoo applied to the wet coat and lathered up briskly will do a splendid job. Be careful not to get the lather into the cat's eyes or ears. Rinse thoroughly, at least twice, pouring the water through the coat with a cup—do not use a spray, for the noise and hiss of the water from the spray will frighten the cat. Dry the cat as well as possible with towels, and then keep him in a warm, dry spot until he is completely dry, and do not expose him to drafts or chill for the next day so that he will not catch cold.

If the bath is beyond your powers, try rubbing white fuller's earth into the coat, or cornmeal, as was done to clean milady's furs in years past. Brush the foreign powder out completely reaching right down to the roots of the hairs with a good, stiff brush. Should the fur appear too dry after brushing and cleaning, a few drops of brilliantine, rubbed into the brush bristles with your hand, will put a shine on the coat. If it appears somewhat greasy at first, do not be alarmed, for it will be absorbed by the fur inside of twenty-four hours. I do not advise doing anything to the coat less than a week before the show. The coat should be left clear, only brushing done the last week unless, of course, the cat, with the usual perversity of the feline tribe, manages to get himself nicely muddied up.

Purely by accident, a friend discovered a means to rid Siamese cats of road-tar without clipping their fur or making them uncomfortable. Sinbad, her old neuter, escaped from the house, ran across the freshly tarred road, and got his feet and lower legs covered with the sticky stuff. After trying various means without success, this intrepid woman solved her vexing problem. She dipped Sinbad's paws, one by one, into a jar partly filled with clear mineral oil, having covered the bottom of his cage with numerous layers of paper. To her great relief, the tar soon dropped off the cat's paws, which were not burned, only irritated. Later she telephoned her successful recipe to her veterinarian, who also applied it successfully.

For a day or two before the show, be very careful about feeding the cat, and do not overfeed—rather, feed less than usual. Nervousness and some fright at shows cause cats to eliminate improperly, and if the digestive tract is full, the cat will develop a bloat which detracts from his appearance. Above all, if there is a specialty on the first day of the show, do not feed the cat until after he has been judged. Put a sign on his cage, clearly printed, large enough to be easily seen, with the notation "DO NOT FEED," and see to it that it is always there when you have to leave him. Unless you take this precaution you are apt to return to take him to the judging ring only to find him finishing a plate of horsemeat, and looking as if he had swallowed a tennis ball at the very least. Many breeders place locks on the cages in the show rooms, but I have always hesitated to do this, for, if an emergency arose, it would be difficult and time-wasting to get the cat out of the cage in the owner's absence.

AT THE SHOW

A good precaution, and one which will protect your cat from the kind pettings and fondlings of strangers, is to cover the front of the cage with a sheet of clear plastic. Moreover, so many people do not understand that males are apt to be rather excited in the show room, due to the presence of other toms and the many strange cats, and that the male is likely to bite fingers thrust into his cage which have upon them the odor of other cats. It would seldom occur to visitors at a dog show to go about petting the entries there, but they seldom think that cats may not welcome their advances. Despite warning signs placed about in most show rooms, visitors will, if the cages are open, put their fingers in, never realizing that, apart from the danger to themselves, they are exposing the cat in the cage to any disease germ floating about. Parents often allow children to do this at shows, and I fear I have offended many a mother's darling by requesting as politely as possible that the child keep hands off.

SHOWING HINTS

The shows have stewards to take cats to the judging ring and return them to their cages when the judging is done, but I find that the Siamese is calmer and better behaved if his owner handles him, and this privilege is extended to owners at most shows. Just before you put your Siamese in the judging pen, groom him with a soft suede glove or a piece of silk cloth, passing the glove or silk from the nose right to the end of the tail several times, and do not neglect to groom down the legs with pressure. This creates a sort of static electricity which causes the hairs to cling to the skin and to each other, giving the cat a nice, sleek appearance. Be sure to wipe out the cor-

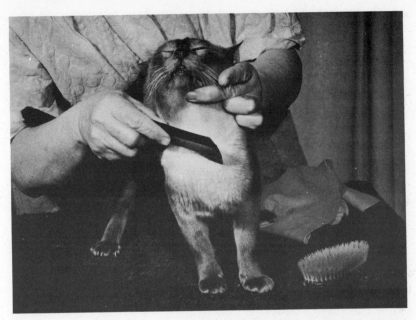

This Blue-Point Siamese, owned by Dr. Smith, loves to be combed and groomed. Combing with a fine-toothed comb should follow brushing.

ners of the cat's eyes, too, and be sure that his nose is clean, and polish the mask with glove or silk, not forgetting the ears.

Some breeders sandpaper the cat's coat, and this is not considered as anything but grooming, but must be done with gentleness to avoid giving the ends of the hairs a singed appearance. If sandpapering is overdone, and the coat is worn down so that spots of thinness appear, the cat will be penalized. Plucking also is done, but this is rather rough treatment, and one I have never used on my cats who are used to very gentle handling.

If the hair on the cat's ears appears thin, some weeks before the show season, rub them with bear grease salve, which will encourage the growth of hair. This is also good, following any sickness, to prevent drying of the hair roots and to aid in preventing the hairs in mask and ears from turning light to due the temperature the cat has run during the course of illness. The temperature will dry out the roots of the hairs, and this will result in paler color and the appearance of "ticking" in the points unless they are lubricated. Care must be taken not to use any form of oil or grease to which the cat may be allergic. The bear grease salve has a faint lemony odor which is not very offensive to the cat. I remember a tragic time we once had with my Petita, who had a lot of light hairs coming into her mask as a result of bearing and nursing kittens. I did so want to show her that fall, for she needed only three points to complete her championship. I got some "baby oil," the same that I had used on my own children when they were tiny, and industriously massaged the oil

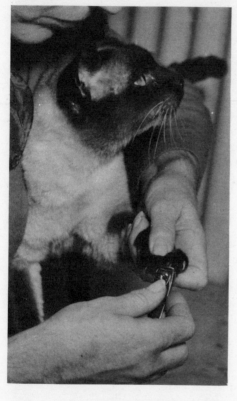

Clip the cat's nails to keep the feet in excellent shape and lend a finished grooming look to the paw.

into poor Tita's face for several days. I thought she was looking a bit strange one morning, and as the day went on, the stranger she appeared. By dinner time that evening, her face was definitely swollen, her eyes becoming like slits and her nose out of all proportion. In frantic haste we took her to the vet, who asked questions until I remembered the oil, and how he laughed. He scrubbed her face with cotton and water, and—horrors—all the hair came off! She was a sight, and not a pretty one. I almost wept. It seems that the baby oil, mild as it was, contained a preservative to which some animals, just like some human babies, have an allergy. Tita, needless to say, was NOT shown. A Siamese with no hair on his face, peering at you with just that spade-shaped area of dark skin showing, is a weird-looking creature.

TRAVELING TO SHOW

For traveling to shows, whether you travel by train, plane, or car, have a good carrier for the cat. Protection from sights and sounds, as far as possible, is necessary for the cat's comfort, but despite the nervous nature of most Siamese, it is amazing how they adjust to strangeness. I thought the noise and roar of plane travel would be very upsetting to the cats, but found that they really did not mind it too much. Train travel is harder because it takes longer. Travel by car is easy, for one can let the cat out of his carrier for a few minutes at a time during a trip, and he feels comforted to know that he can be with you for awhile, at any rate. Line the carrier heavily with white paper towels or something of that sort—not newspapers, for of late we find that the newsprint ink comes off and dirties the cat's coat—and put a soft cotton or wool blanket over half the papers. This will take care of sanitary needs, and the papers can easily be changed at any time. The blanket is a comfort to him and provides a soft spot for a nap. Have a dish handy, a saucer that you can put water in, for cats are thirsty creatures, to whom a drink of water is very welcome on a trip.

CAGES AND DECORATION

The cages used at the shows are not always the same size, so the problem of hangings for the cage is rather complicated. Hangings made with drawstrings through the top, which can be adjusted to fit any cage just by gathering the string, are the most convenient type to use. Part-wool blankets, the new plastics, or any warm and clean flexible material in a pretty color will do.

I have lately made hangings of a lovely shade of blue oilcloth, with the cattery name, "Ebon Mask", done in white enamel on the middle twenty inches of the long piece of material. About the edges we put rivets and through these the hanging is hooked to the top of the cage from end to end, the hooks having had all sharpness removed by clipping off the piercing end of the hooks. If the cage is small, we just turn in the ends of the hangings. Floor mats to match make a neat-appearing cage, but the cat should always have a pillow or blanket which is soft and warm. Extra floor coverings are always taken along, for, although a cat may be perfectly trained at home, it is strange how he will unaccountably become "unhousebroken" at the shows, and use the floor covering instead of the pan.

Red is a popular color for decorations for Siamese cages, and it does look lovely against the warm tone. I prefer blue personally: it matches their eyes and sets off the coats very well. Gold, not yellow, but a soft gold, is another color that makes an attractive background for the Siamese, and a soft rose is lovely for the Blue-Points.

Whatever color you use, be sure the hangings are made of washable material, for they should be washed and aired after each show, and hung out in the sun for a day after being cleaned. If the cat is to be left in the showroom overnight, he'll be happy if he has his carrier in which to sleep, where he'll be safe from chills or drafts. Leave the carrier open and have a blanket in it, and he'll put in a restful night. Some hotels allow cats in the rooms, but it never seems fair to me to take a tomcat into a hotel room, for he may spray and that odor is not easy to banish, especially if the tom should spray on the wallpaper or carpets. Better to leave the males in their cages, and if you must have a cat for company (and who doesn't?), take a female to the room with you.

It's a good idea to take your own dishes for feeding the cat. The shows use paper dishes, and I always expect to see a cat eat the dish as well as the meat, for the paper does soak up the meat flavor. Leaving a dish of water in the cage is not a very bright idea, for the cat will undoubtedly, just when you want him to look his best, dip his tail into the water, or upset the dish and get himself all messy and wet. Rather, put the saucer in every couple of hours, and give him a chance to have drink frequently.

When you return home from a show, if possible, isolate the cat from the others who have remained at home. If he has picked up any infection, this precaution will protect the others. Give his coat a cleaning with a disinfectant, and feed him carefully for a few days, not overfeeding. Watch to see that bowel functions are normal, and that he shows no signs of illness before allowing him loose with the rest of the feline family.

Happenings at shows will take their accustomed course, and you,

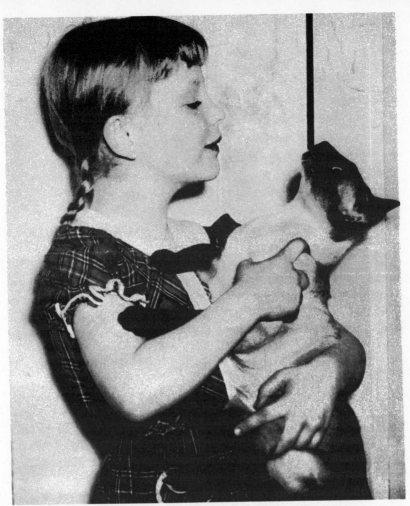

Lucia Jane Stackhouse is shown with Doneraile Dandie.
A champion, Dandie was imported from the English
breeder, Mrs. K. R. Williams and is owned by Mr. and
Mrs. Howard Stackhouse of Mt. Holly, New Jersey.

Dr. Fern Smith's Champion Blue-Point Siamese with some of the ribbons and trophies this fine animal has won.

if you are inexperienced at showing, will learn quickly if you follow the lead of some breeder who has several entries in the show. Listen closely, once judging of your breed has begun, for your class to be called, and for your cat's individual number. It's extremely irritating to the judge, and to other exhibitors, to be forced to wait for some cat to be brought to the judging ring long after the rest of the class has been ready for judging. Sit back and take it easy, enjoy the judging despite the butterflies in your tummy, and if you watch the judge's handling and especially listen carefully to any comments the judge may make (for some judges do talk while they handle the animals, and explain why one goes up and another down) you'll learn a lot. If you don't win one year, try again, and keep moving along; don't stand still with the same cats for years, but progress and bring out better ones each season. Your first win of "Best in Show" will repay you for all your efforts. You'll float on little pink clouds, with stars about your head, and your cat will act quite unconcerned, but you won't be able to be so blasé. It's a grand and glorious feeling, I

140

Triple Champion Barton Ridge Liebling, Blue-Point male.
Owned and bred by Alice Hahn of North Haven, Con-
necticut, Liebling, in 1957, won the A.C.F.A. and the
Cats Magazine awards of, All Northeastern Honorable
Mention Blue-Point male, and All Eastern Honorable
Mention Blue-Point male respectively.

promise you. May you all experience it once or more in your exhibiting career.

FAMOUS SHOW WINNERS

For fifty years Siamese have been exhibited in this country, and they have come a long way from the early specimens to those of the present. The type has changed decidedly for the better due to the great interest and scientific approach to breeding taken by the serious exhibitors and breeders. I'll try to give you the names of some of the truly outstanding cats of the past and present. Back in the thirties there was a Blue-Pointed male, Ch. Wun Lon Song, bred and owned by the late Mrs. Karl Norton of "Siam" cattery fame. Mrs. Norton herself was a leading light in the fancy and is sorely missed by all of us. Many of the good Blue-Points of American breeding have this male's name in their pedigrees. His son Ch. Siam's Chief Noda Purachatr was also a famous sire. Ch. Wan Tutsawan, bred and owned by Miss Elsa Wunderlich, was perhaps

Grand Champion Chi Charoen Pada was awarded the "All-American Seal-Point Female" honor in 1955. She has been the mother of four Siamese champions, and one of her children became a double and grand champion.

142

the outstanding female Blue-Pointed Siamese over a period of many years, often taking "Best Champion" in show over all breeds, an unusual honor in days when the Siamese were not so numerous as now. Mrs. R. Hecht's Gr. Ch. Vee Roi's Lantara Gene, a female of exquisite coloring, has been "Best in Show" so many times it is amazing. Mrs. Alexander Pinney's Blue-Points, Ch. Rasna's Huios and Ch. Rasna's Ilo, son and grandson of her Rasna's Clensi, have made their mark in show annals. Clensi was fifteen years old when he died, had sired well over 500 kittens, and had champions galore to his credit. Chirn Sa-Hai cattery, owned by Mrs. Beth O'Donovan, has produced so many well-known cats that one can name only a small number of them as representative—Ch. Cha Wah Chirn Sa-Hai, Ch. Hansa, Ch. Dahling, Ch. Zombie, Gr. Ch. Nee Yang, etc.

The name "Newton" needs no introduction to the breeders, for Mrs. Arthur Cobb's prefix has made its own fame. Ch. Oriental Nanki Poo of Newton, Imp., has champion off-spring in all parts of this land; among them several grand champions. Hollycat Cattery, owned by Mr. and Mrs. Howard Stackhouse, has produced many show winners; among them the never-to-be-forgotten Ch. Hollycat Blue Micky, an outstandingly beautiful Blue-Pointed male. Catteries which have made names for themselves are too numerous to mention individually, but some are so familiar to the breeders that they deserve a particular note here.

They include: Millbrook, owned by Mr. and Mrs. Walter Roose; Cymri, owned by Mrs. L. Pedull Blue Grass, Mrs. Lucas Combs; Shawnee, Mrs. N. Horner; Pomonock, Mrs. Julia Kohlus; Siama, Mrs. LaVern Chapman; Chi Charoen, Mrs. German; Kwan Yin, Mr. and Mrs. Deeths and Mr. and Mrs. Wilson; Dalai, Mrs. W. Daly; our own Ebon Mask suffix, and so many more that one cannot list them all. These breeders raise all colors of Siamese—Seal, Blue, Chocolate and Frost-Pointed cats—some specializing, as we do, in one color, others breeding all kinds.

Importations have become so numerous of recent years that it would take a book to list all, but such cattery names as Prestwick, Oriental, Doneraile, Holmesdale, Sukianga, Spotlight, Balhaven, Briarry, Southwood, Silken, Quesi, and Quantock are becoming almost as familiar as the American names. With these to help us we should produce better cats each season. The show entries become larger each year and the popularity of the Siamese does not wane

Bred from fine stock this half grown Siamese kitten shows evidence of the future beauty he will attain at maturity.

The Siamese dearly loves its scratching post.

with increasing numbers but seems rather to be growing by leaps and bounds.

It is impossible to write of everything pertaining to the Siamese; indeed, nobody can make claim to complete knowledge of the Siamese cat. The information in this book is a collection of items gathered through years of breeding and handling Siamese, as well as from kindly and thoughful contacts with veterinarians and breeders who helped us over our early troubles. Knowledge also has been gained by direct experience, a hard but a thorough teacher. The breeding of Siamese is a hobby, dear not only to the writer but to the entire family. As I have written this, each member of the family has said, "Mama, have you told them this—or that?" What I have omitted is not by intention, and I hope that what is here will help, for that was the purpose of this collection of facts and fancies in the first place. May you prosper in your attempts to breed better Siamese, more of you each day and year, is my sincere wish.

The family tree of any cat, the genetic qualities given it
by its forebears, will mold the animal to specific form
and function.

CHAPTER 11

GENETICS OF THE SIAMESE CAT

by A. C. Jude

THE science of genetics, which is comparatively modern, has received ever-increasing attention during the past fifty or sixty years. The amount of knowledge made available has been of the utmost value to physiologists, pathologists and others similarly engaged, and to a host of people whose interests are vested in the various branches of animal breeding. We have been able to note many advances in the treatment of disease and deformity; the creditable increases in both quality and performance of all farm animals; and we have watched with admiration the evolving of new breeds and varieties to suit many special requirements. These successes have, to a large extent, been made possible by the use of the newly acquired knowledge. Nowadays, too, it is accepted that the small-livestock fancier will benefit if he will but study certain aspects of the science, and combine its facts with the art of selection. It is because of these conditions that the author of this book decided to include this new chapter.

It happens from time to time that fanciers without knowledge of the scientific side of breeding will produce winners. When this happens it is quickly asserted that here is proof that scientific knowledge is unnecessary. It is usually found, however, that these breeders are new to a fancy, and that they have purchased well-bred stock and merely reproduced from the stage already reached by some experienced breeder. We do not suggest for a moment that a really deep knowledge of the science is necessary for the average fancier, but we do believe that if the basic principles are studied and used, the fancier will meet with more certain and continued success, and will be able to enjoy his efforts and experiences to a far greater degree. To say the very least, it is always far more interesting to know why a thing happens than merely that it just does!

The facts of heredity have given us a fresh conception of the individual. So far, we had been accustomed to distinguish between the members of a family by assigning to each an individuality, and by making use of certain external features (such as coat color or markings)

These kittens have developed their dark points and are beginning to show evidence of the characteristics they inherited from their parents.

to express the individuality of these different animals. Otherwise, our idea of what constituted individuality in each case was vague. Now, instead of looking at an individual as a whole, vaguely marked off from its fellows, we are able to see him in terms of definite and built-up characters, depending primarily upon the number and variety of the factors that existed in the two gametes (sexual cells) that went into his building.

The presence or absence of a comparatively small number of factors in a species carries with it the possibility of an enormous range of individual variations. In every instance the variation depends on the presence or absence of the definite factors carried by the gametes from whose union the individual results. And as these factors separate out cleanly in the gametes which the individual forms, such variations as depend on them are transmitted strictly according to the Mendelian scheme. If the constitution of the gametes is unchanged, the heredity of such variation is independent of any change in the conditions of nutrition, or other environment, which may operate upon the individual producing the gametes.

VARIATIONS

Everyone knows that animals often react quite clearly to their environmental conditions. This is particularly evident in the characters of size and weight. There is no evidence, however, that the effects of changed conditions are connected with alteration in the nature of the gametes which the individual produces. We can say, therefore, that there are two sorts of variations: those which are due to heredity, and those which are due to environment. The first are known as mutations, and the second can be termed fluctuations, for which at present there is no valid reason for supposing them ever to be inherited. There are cases, of course, where one might be led to feel that heredity plays a part, as for instance with some small kittens from undernourished cats. It is natural to attribute the smaller size of the offspring to some genetic factor, but the fact remains that this need have nothing to do with heredity. The kittens draw their nourishment from the mother in their pre-natal state, and their size is affected because the poorly-nourished parent offered bad environment for the kittens, and not because the gametes were changed by the adverse conditions. This parent is not only the producer of gametes but is also the environment of her kittens, and it is in the latter capacity that it has affected its offspring. The entire difference

Both of these Siamese cats were modeled by man; the ceramic one by his hands, the live one by his knowledge of genetics.

between the two variations in their causation gives a clear view of the process of evolution. Darwin pointed out that any theory of evolution must be based on the facts of heredity and variation. But to be of any moment in evolutionary changes, a variation must be inherited; and to be inherited, it must be represented in the gametes.

When the fancier takes a hand in the guiding of the hereditary process, he works with variable animals, some of which may be particularly variable because of some complex multiple pedigree. Variations come along which seem desirable to the fancier. He pairs variants which are similar. He eliminates undesirables, brings similar forms together as pairs, and prevents crossing with other breeds or varieties. The reason why the fancier can work more quickly than nature in reaching a given end, is simply that he can control the pairing. He has complete control over form, color, and health, working all together to produce his ideal. But we must realize that man cannot create—he merely operates with the variations which occur.

Quite obviously, one cannot in a single chapter hope to give more than a brief outline of the subject as a whole, so the object must be to present the more important parts, and try to arouse an interest which will prompt the reader to follow up on the subject through reading in specialized works. There are a number of branches to the subject, but here we shall confine our observations mainly to the matters relating to reproduction, for we believe that cat breeders need as much information as possible about how their pets reproduce, and how variations or changes can be brought about, which will eventually produce individuals who will more nearly conform to some given standard of color or type than that displayed by the parents of their ancestry.

THE EGG AND THE SPERM

One observation concerning heredity seems accepted generally, namely, that "like begets like." Even those who suggest they have no use for the scientific breeding knowledge, almost instinctively follow the maxim which is basically correct. They match up their pairs of breeding stock so as to produce an anticipated harmony of likeness to the parents. This then brings us to discussion of the seats of origin of likeness—the egg and the sperm.

Of the many differences between male and female, the most essential is in the reproductive organs. The female germ cell is known as the ovum, and the male germ cell as spermatozoon. A union of the two through the piercing of the ovum by the head of the spermatozoon is termed fertilization, and it is by this very simple process that the new life begins, a life which is to carry the complete and complex combination of characteristics of the two individuals who have contributed the sexual cells or gametes. This new life is technically

Cells in the process of division.

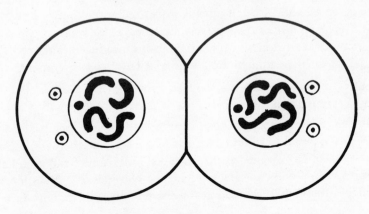

151

known as a zygote. Since a zygote is formed by the fusion of two separate gametes, this new individual must be regarded throughout its life as a double structure in which the components brought in by each of the gametes remain intimately fused in a form of partnership. But when the zygote in its turn comes to form gametes, the partnership is broken and the process is reversed. The component parts of the dual structure are resolved with the formation of a set of single structures, the gametes. If we put it another way, we may say that every cat has a double hereditary equipment, one passed on by the sire, one passed on by the dam. And when a cat forms ova or sperm as the case may be, the hereditary equipment has to be brought down to the simplex state, so that when a mother germ cell comes to form daughter cells, each daughter cell receives the necessary equipment in the simplex state, one set of factors being passed on to one daughter, the other set to the other daughter. Whether these daughter cells develop into eggs or sperms, the point to note is that the hereditary equipment of each is in the simplex state.

In crosses between different breeds or varieties of cats we are able to follow the inheritance of such special features as long or short hair, large or small ears, and so on. Each special character is conditioned by a gene. The gene is the unit of heredity—the physicial basis of inherited characteristics. It is a material body located within a particular chromosome of the nucleus of germ cells, and from them is handed on directly to the body cells which arise from the germ cells in development. It is believed that genes are arranged in a definite order on the chromosomes, and genes situated in the same place on corresponding chromosomes all affect the same characteristic. The egg, however, is not merely a container of chromosomes. The cytoplasm of the egg is already organized at the time of fertilization. Its parts differ qualitatively, so that as cleavage progresses, blastomeres with different potentialities are produced, although the nuclei which they contain are all alike in chromosome content.

CELL DIVISION

At cell division each of the chromosomes splits longitudinally. Half of each passes to the opposite end of the cell, and there the halves coalesce to build two new nuclei. The cell pulls in half and each half contains one of the two new nuclei. The chromosome splits longitudinally; therefore, each half gets a share of every hereditary factor

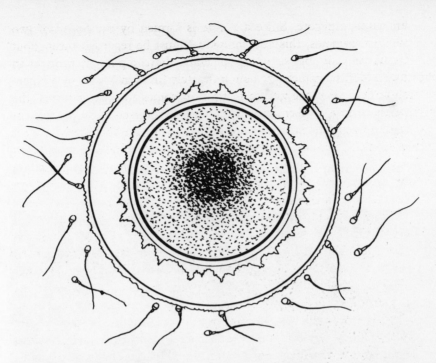

An egg is a special giant cell produced by the female ovaries. Here sperm are assaulting the egg in an effort to pierce the protective envelope that surrounds it. Once inside the sperm will lose its tail, fertilize the egg, and bring fifty percent of the chromosomes to match the fifty percent already present in the dark nucleus of the egg, making a normal cell number. Growth enzymes surround the nucleus of the egg.

Chromosomes in
nucleus of cell

Chromosomes arranged in
pairs, showing partnership

on that chromosome. Imagine what happens when fertilization of an egg by a sperm takes place. If each cell contained the full complement of chromosomes, every cell in the embryo would contain twice the number of chromosomes of the cells of both mother and father; then in each generation the number of chromosomes would double itself. But this does not happen because the chromosomes exist in identical pairs in cells.

When an egg and sperm are being formed by multiplication of certain parent cells in the sex organs during the final cell division, instead of the chromosome splitting, one of each half goes to each

A good Seal-Point Siamese stud cat, Dalai Jakki.

end of the cell; therefore, the two new cells which are formed, and which are to be eggs and sperms, contain only half the normal number of chromosomes. Thus, when fertilization takes place again, the original number of chromosomes is produced.

CHROMOSOMES

The chromosomes of the mother may contain different hereditary factors from the chromosomes of the father. For example, the mother's chromosomes may carry factors for long hair, and the father's chromosomes may carry factors for short hair. Alternatively, the reverse may be the case—the mother's chromosomes may carry the factors for short hair, and the father's chromosomes may carry the factors for long hair. In either case, a mating will produce always the same result—kittens which all will be short-haired. It is for that reason that we say short-coated is dominant to long-coated, which is termed recessive. For convenience sake, we call this first generation the F1. From what has already been written it will be understood that although these first generation kittens all exhibit short-coatedness they do, in fact, carry a factor for long-coatedness. If now we mate two of these short-coated kittens together, we shall produce in this F2 generation three kittens who will exhibit short-coatedness to every one who will exhibit long-coatedness. Of the three short-coated kittens, one will be pure for the factor (carrying it in duplex), and the other two will be hybrids (carrying only one factor for the recessive). The other kitten will be long-coated because it carries the factor for long-coatedness in duplex. It is found that in every normal case where the inheritance of an alternative pair of characters is concerned, the effect of the cross in successive generations is to produce three, and only three, different sorts of individuals, viz. dominants which breed true, dominants which give both dominant and recessive offspring in the ratio 3:1, and recessives which always breed true. It is possible to put the theory to a further test. The explanation of the 3:1 ratio of dominants and recessives in the F2 generation is regarded as due to the F1 individuals producing equal numbers of gametes bearing the dominant and recessive elements respectively. If now the F1 offspring be mated with the pure recessive, we are bringing together a series of gametes consisting of equal numbers of dominants and recessives with a series consisting solely of recessives. We ought from such a cross to obtain equal numbers of dominant and recessive individuals, and further, the dominants as produced ought all to give both dominants and recessives in the ratio 3:1 when they themselves are bred. Both these expectations can be confirmed, and crossing with the recessive is now a recognized way of testing whether an animal bearing a dominant character is a pure dominant or an impure dominant which is carrying the recessive character. In the former case the offspring will be all of

Cats and kids go together, especially if the cat is a Siamese. The temperament and trainability of your cat are also inherited characteristics.

the dominant form, while in the latter they will consist on the average of equal numbers of dominants and recessives.

So far, we have examined the situation where only a single pair of characters is involved, and we have seen that from a crossing we can expect a ratio of three dominants to one recessive in the F2 generation. The same proportion (3:1) is expected when an increased number of pairs of characters is involved, and therefore, although a little more complicated, we are able to forecast the results of any mating, provided we know the genetic constitution of the parents, and which factors are dominant or recessive. Thus, for example, when a long-coated black cat is crossed with a Seal-Pointed Siamese, we have two pairs of characters—long coat, short coat; full black, and restriction. Short coat is dominant over long coat; full color is dominant over restriction. So our F2 result will be nine short-coated blacks, three long-coated blacks; three short-coated S. P. Siamese, one long-coated S. P. Siamese. The 3:1 ratio is followed through. In a further increase of characters our F2 figures would be extended to 27, 9, 9, 9, 3, 3, 3, 1; and so on.

THE SEX CHROMOSOMES

So much for the chromosomes which carry the factors for the various inherited chracteristics. Two chromosomes, however, are sex chromosomes. In the female they are similar, and are known as "X" chromosomes; but in the male they are different, one is called "X" chromosome, the other "Y". It will be realized from this that when the eggs are being formed by the female, only eggs bearing "Y" chromosomes are formed. But when the sperms of the male are produced, half of these will contain an "X" chromosome, and half will contain a "Y" chromosome. So if an "X" sperm fertilizes an egg, two "X" chromosomes come together and a female offspring is the result. On the other hand, should a "Y" sperm fertilize an egg, an "X" and a "Y" chromosome come together and the offspring is a male. As a general rule, the cross between a male and a female results in the production of the two sexes in approximately equal numbers where large numbers of litters are brought into account. But there are cases where a different position is operative, and the case of the tortoiseshell cat is a classic example. Here, when a yellow female is mated with a black male, the male kittens are yellow, and the females are tortoiseshell. When these are mated together, we expect yellow females, tortoiseshell females, yellow males, and black males. In the reciprocal cross, i.e. black female crossed yellow male, we get tortoiseshell females, and black males, and when these are crossed, we expect black females, tortoiseshell females, black males, and yellow males; no tortoiseshell males except in rare instances.

EMBRYONIC GROWTH

A brief description of how the youngsters are carried by a queen will be of interest. The uterus, with its two appendages or horns as they are technically named, is an organ shaped like a tuning fork, the handle representing the womb proper, and the two prongs corresponding to the two appendages. In the case of mammals whose general habit is to bear only one offspring, the uterus continues to grow as pregnancy advances, whilst the tubes remain small. In the case of those mammals which produce a number of youngsters at each pregnancy, the uterus does not function in the same way, and carries no young, its purpose being taken over by the tubes which extend up around each flank of the female. In the cat, the walls of the tube are very thin, so thin in fact, as to be almost transparent. Each youngster is encased in a small sac, the walls of which are also extremely thin, while each unborn youngster is attached to the wall of the tube by a tiny disc-shaped organ called the placenta. Leading from the placenta is a cord which enters the youngster's body at the umbilicus. The cord contains blood vessels which convey blood to and from the placenta, and it is by means of the placenta that the interchange takes place between the dam and offspring; the waste products from the offspring being transferred to the circulation of the dam through the placenta, while the placenta also absorbs and passes on to the youngster the elements necessary for life and growth. In other words, the placenta is an organ of exchange, and has to function as stomach, lung, and kidney for the young, developing organism. The tubes in which the youngsters are carried, as has already been mentioned, are so thin-walled that they must occupy a minor role during labor, and part of their function in this respect is taken over by the muscles of the abdomen and the diaphragm, the latter being a dome-shaped muscular organ which divides the chest from the abdomen. This explains why, when a queen is carrying quite a large litter, labor is slow and difficult—the muscles of the abdomen being over-extended, lose tone and power, and in consequence the apparatus for expulsion is considerably impaired.

Your Siamese loves to play with a catnip mouse and, through the exercise it provides, this play helps the cat to attain to his muscular heritage.

The new life, which in our observations has been formed, is now growing in its prenatal stage, and will soon be relying to considerable extent on self-existence, with all the potentialities for the exhibiting or carrying of the various modified characteristics which were anticipated by the fancier as an outcome of his art of selection. It is about now that success or failure may begin to show.

POST-NATAL GROWTH

Quite separately from genetical differences, the post-natal growth of the sucking youngster is influenced by the several environmental factors concerned, and the main one is the amount of milk available. The mammary glands, although not directly concerned with the reproductive processes, are dependent upon the ovaries for their growth and for the initiation of their functional activity. They consist of milk-secreting tissue surrounded by a fibrous envelope, and for each separate gland there is a sinus or cistern for storing the milk, and communicating with the exterior by a teat. The milk secreted by one gland passes out through the corresponding teat, and cannot be transferred to the ducts of another gland, but the constituents may be reabsorbed, and pass into the blood. The actual amount of milk available varies with the efficiency of the mother's lactation, and the number of young who have to share the quantity. This subject has been studied in great detail, and has been reported on from time to time in the scientific journals. It was shown by Enzmann (1933) **Anat.: Reg.: 56,** 345–358, that the amount of milk produced increases with the number of youngsters sucking, but not proportionately. It was also demonstrated convincingly by MacDowell, Gates, and MacDowell (1930) **J. Gen.: Physiol.: 13,** 529–545, that reduction of litter size favorably affects the remaining individuals. Milk production depends also on maternal age, parity, diet, etc., and in addition, there are innate differences due to heredity. There is an association between sterility and the high probability that the few young born will die of starvation within a few days of birth—if by sterility we mean failure to form embryos. It has become abundantly clear in work on this subject that there is indeed a connection between small size of litter and starvation of litter, but it is associated also with the death of embryos late in gestation. It is a queen who has a dead embryo or embryos, and consequently a placenta still in position instead of being torn away, who fails to have a good milk supply. Furthermore, it occurs only when death is fairly late in pregnancy— say in the second half. It is believed that a stock which has small litters (i.e. a low number of eggs released by the ovary), may suckle perfectly well, but a stock in which a proportion of the embryos dies late in gestation whether for genetic or other reasons, may be very poor milkers.

Kittens mirror the genetic qualities behind them. Thus a knowledge of the faults and virtues of the animals in their pedigree gives the breeder a good idea of what to expect from the kittens.

Head study of a lovely Siamese owned by Dallas Sidlo.
Glory - S - Sherry is a Red-Point and is a U.C.F. champion and A.C.F.A. quadruple champion.

GLANDS AND HORMONES

Essential to the well-being of the body is the proper adjustment of the various systems, one to the other. For instance, growth in the cat takes place over approximately one year, or in some breeds, perhaps a little more. After this time, slowing down occurs, which is combined with a development of the sex organs. So that the two processes may not become disproportionate, the body is provided with a series of glands known as the endocrine system. These glands have the function of pouring their secretions directly into the blood instead of opening into some particular organ by way of a duct. For this reason these glands are known as ductless glands. The chief of these glands are the thyroid, parathyroid, adrenals, the islets of Langerhans, pituitary and the gonads (testes and ovaries). The secretions of any of these glands are spoken of as hormones, whose work it is to stimulate a particular organ.

Standing is the Seal-Point female, Grand Champion Newton's Jay Tee, breeder-owner, Mrs. Arthur Cobb, Newton, Massachusetts. In the foreground is another Seal-Point female, Champion Chindwin's Singumin of Newton, bred by Mr. E. Battey, and owned by Mrs. Arthur Cobb.

A litter of ten kittens, a phenomenal number particularly for Siamese. The breeder, Mrs. J. H. Dingwerth (Meru Cattery), was justly proud of this huge litter and the evident quality of all the kits. They are by Meru Shang-Ti x Meru Devadassi. The kits were about seven weeks of age when the photo was taken.

Perhaps the most important of these glands from the fancier's point of view are the pituitary and thyroid which concern growth; and the gonads and thymus which concern the sexual characteristics. The pituitary has two lobes, each with three distinct functions: the posterior lobe regulates the flow of urine, causes contractions necessary at birth, and has some influence on blood pressure. The anterior lobe regulates growth, controls sexual development, and has some stimulating effect on milk production. There are two substances (hormones) elaborated in the anterior pituitary gland which when reaching the blood stream act on the ovary. The first, (follicle-stimulating hormone) stimulates the follicle to ripen, and the second (lutealising hormone) causes the follicles to rupture and to form corpora lutea. The anterior pituitary gland of mares is particularly rich in the first hormone, and that of cows and ewes rich in the second. Substances similar to these are now obtained commercially from other sources. These are sold by druggists under various trade names, and the dosage is calculated in international units (I. U.). Underfunctioning of the pituitary leads to dwarfism and sexual underdevelopment known as infantilism. Overfunctioning of the pituitary during early life leads to an obese condition. A condition of adiposity is a very common cause of infertility. Very fat animals do not come into season in a very marked way, and when they do so, the periods are apt to be irregular and likely to be missed, or the animals may fail to breed altogether. The relation between fatness and infertility, however, is not always a simple one of cause and effect. Underdevelopment of the reproductive organs or a mere postponement of breeding may themselves lead to an overly fat condition, and females, if fed too well before their first service, may prove infertile for a prolonged period. Again, good feeding favors an early puberty, but if animals are not bred reasonably early, the chances of subsequent sterility at a time when it is desired that they should have progeny, are increased. In order to favor continuous fertility, female animals should be encouraged to breed regularly. If this is not done, the normal functional activity of the ovaries is liable to be deranged, owing to the tissues becoming overloaded with an excessive number of luteal scars arising from the follicles that have discharged their ova without being fertilized. Thus the chances of sterility are always increased in an animal that has not been bred from over a prolonged period, since the ovarian rhythm is thereby interfered with, and the cyclical ripening and rupture of the follicles do not necessarily occur.

SECONDARY SEX CHARACTERISTICS

The male character in any animal is denoted by the appearance and shape of certain parts of the body, in particular those of the head and neck. While most breeders require these characters to be well marked, they are of themselves no criterion of the breeding efficiency of the animal; for although they are dependent upon an internal secretion of the testes, the latter may be formed quite independently of the production of spermatozoa. In certain breeds, these secondary sexual characters are much more marked than in others; nevertheless, the breeds in which the secondary characters are only slightly developed, are quite as fertile as those in which the sex differences are well developed. It is a common mistake among breeders to suppose that because a male animal is potent, therefore it is fertile. It not infrequently happens that a male animal may be able to perform the sexual act and eject fluid from the generative glands and yet be incapable of impregnating owing to absence of spermatozoa from the ejaculate. Deficiency of spermatozoa is sometimes due to inbreeding. When it is only temporary, as sometimes happens, it is more likely to occur in early and in later life rather than

The ultimate results of good and knowledgeable breeding practice — fine specimens beautiful enough to show and win top awards.

in the middle period. Moreover, with young males it is inadvisable to allow service to occur too often even though the service is fertile, as frequent service when performed too early is likely to result in the under-development of the sire, and to impair his breeding capacity in later life. Young males are most likely to suffer from under-feeding and over-use, whereas old males suffer from over-feeding and under-use.

Occasionally in males the testes do not descend into the scrotum but are retained in the abdomen, their situation in foetal life. Such animals usually still have the external appearance of males and are mostly capable of service, but are almost always sterile. It may be mentioned that sperms are very susceptible to high temperatures, and the scrotum is a device for keeping the testes at a lower temperature than the body. Where one testis only is retained, the animal may be perfectly fertile, but it is inadvisable to breed from such animals, as the condition is likely to be inherited.

The belief that a purebred female which has once been served a by mongrel male will be apt to produce in the future when mated with a purebred male, offspring that are tainted by the mongrel male (telegony), has no foundation in fact; and all critical experiments have failed to prove the assertion. A female that produces a litter

Double Champion Meru Malarky. The photo of this female was taken when she was about five weeks pregnant.

may, however, produce young from two different males to which she has been mated during the heat period, but if one of these males is of the same breed as the female, those young which have been produced by the fusing of his spermatozoa with the ova of the female will be purebred; this is owing to the fact that only one spermatozoon can unite with an ovum, and once it is fertilized, no other sperm has any effect on it.

It is sometimes said that it is dangerous to mate a small female with a large male because of difficulties in parturition. Some recent experiments with horses have shown, however, that the mother controls the size of the young to such size as she can bear. That is, reciprocal crosses between Shetland ponies and Shire horses made by artificial insemination have shown that through nutrition during pregnancy and the suckling period, the dam controls the growth of the foal to a much greater extent than the sire.

LETHAL GENES

Certain genes occur in many kinds of animals which result in death in the pre-natal state or early in the post-natal condition. These genes are known as lethal genes. They cause the death of the individual when in homozygous state, though in a heterozygous state they may have no serious effect. Cause of death is probably inability of the organism to perform certain vital functions. A dominant lethal alters the phenotype when heterozygous, but kills it when homozygous. A recessive lethal has no observable effect when heterozygous but kills when homozygous, just as a dominant lethal does. The big snag about many of these lethals is that they produce small effects when present in a single dose. For this reason, these lethals may soon be spread in a fancy. In some of the fancies, a breed of animal carrying only one dose of a certain lethal may be looked upon as a desirable. An instance is the Black-eyed White of the mouse fancy. All the black-eyed Whites are naturally crossbreeds, for all the pures die before birth, but the fancy accepts these hybrids as a breed. Obviously, recessive lethals are not easy to detect in mammals, because one has to deduce their existence from the absence of a quarter of the offspring. While it would be easy to notice the absence of, say, a hundred flies from among four hundred, it is not so easy to notice the absence of a quarter of a litter of cats. No known list of lethals in the cat has been published, but tail-lessness and polydactylism are likely involved. For those interested in the subject

The Frost-Point, imported male, Quadruple Champion Laurentide Thio Imp, was All-American in 1958 and All-Midwestern in 1957-1958. He is owned by Madeleine Christy.

there was a paper by C. H. Danforth on polydactylism in the **J. of Hed**: about 1946, and the subject of lethals is touched on by H. S. Jennings in **Genetics;** by Darlington in **Evolution of Genetic Systems;** and in Altenberg's **Genetics.**

Besides genes, which are lethal, there are others which have effects harmful to the organism, but not necessarily fatal. These effects frequently take the form of what are known as hereditary diseases, and so may be termed pathological effects. Such effects in mammals may be manifested in a variety of organs and ways, affecting either the nervous system and the sense organs, the muscular system, the blood system including the heart, the excretory system (kidneys), or the reproductive system.

HOW TO IMPROVE STOCK

To improve one's stock, systematic breeding is necessary. Anything in breeding which is haphazard is useless, and can, at the very best, only result in lucky, isolated successes. Because the factors for characteristics are passed jointly from the parents to the offspring, it will be clear that any of the characters concerned will be most readily and most strongly brought to the surface by brother-to-sister matings. But that is only the beginning of the story, for just as the

A nice head portrait of the stud Seal-Point Siamese, Ling, owned by the Palos Verdes Bird Farm, California.

good points are brought to the surface, so are the bad ones. Therefore, except in very highly selected stock which is being used for some quite special purpose, continued brother-to-sister matings would not lead far—the good, and the bad, would still be combined. Just as the closest relationships produce characters in fullest effect, so the more distant ones produce in less effect, and it is this fact which allows us to select from relationships (often fairly far removed), the most suitable ones which, as pairs, will tend to retain the good points and lose the bad ones. Unfortunately, a pair of animals can only transmit through the generations the best of what they, themselves, possess. Any improvement on this "best" must come from outside the family circle—in other words, from a suitably selected outcross. So although we may say that some form of inbreeding is a distinct advantage, but not necessarily close inbreeding, we do have to take into account a wise selection of outcrosses. These, at times, are a matter of necessity—for some further improvement of some particular factor: for an increase of stamina; for assistance in removing unwanted recessives; in the starting or establishing of a new breed, etc. But please realize that continued outcrossing is not a system in itself. To the fancier I would say: your success must depend on ruthless selection and the use of only the healthiest and best, with very special attention paid to all the aspects of efficient reproductive capacity. For this purpose every detail of performance of every animal bred and used must be fully and faithfully recorded, and in the case of animals purchased, strict inquiry must be made into the history of all ancestry recorded by name on the pedigree. Be just as critical of the female as of the male, for although the male mates many females and thus leaves his stamp on many progeny and should therefore be the best and healthiest possible, it should be remembered that the biggest winner in females in a season was produced by a female who probably produced only one-tenth of the progeny sired by a male in the season.

Although recessive factors may remain in a stock through many generations, most of the necessary information concerning an animal can be gleaned from an investigation into the performance of the various individuals named on the pedigree forms used by fanciers. An animal in the fifth ancestral generation contributes only about three per cent of the inheritance of a kitten; beyond that, effects are usually comparatively small. I would end these notes on breeding (and obviously they can here be only notes) by once more drawing particular attention to the necessity for selecting for breeding only those animals who are one hundred percent healthy and reproductive. That is far more important to ultimate success than either type or color.

CAT COLORING

Present-day cat colorings all originated from the well-nown agouti coat pattern, types of which were expressed by a number of wild species crossed from time to time with small wild cats in different countries. At least three types of tabby pattern are traceable. The original tabby markings are still visible as "ghost" patterns in a number of present-day self-colored coats, especially in young animals. The origin of the "striped" pattern of tabby has been traced to the European or the African wildcat. Lined cats occur in both Africa and Europe, and are known as African, Caffre, or Abyssinian. The stripes are fine and close together, except on the legs, tail, and nose. The first impression is of a uniform agouti cat, but it has a dark vertebral line. It is probably from this that the present Abyssinian fancy type was evolved.

The only color pigments found in cats are black, brown, and yellow.

No red pigment as such is present, although yellow is intensified to "red" on the one hand, and reduced to cream on the other. If the pattern factor is "lost" and replaced by the factor of "self," the three pigments freely intermingle. Black, being the densest, overshadows the brown and the yellow, and in consequence, the cat will have a coat black in color. The gene for brown is recessive to its normal allelomorph black. For brown, the oxidation of the melanin pigment does not proceed to its highest state which is black, but stops short at brown. The main effect of the brown gene seems to be reduction of pigment granule size, not number. "Silver" represents a reduction of yellow and of black. Smokes therefore are dark silvers. Doncaster (1912) concluded that yellow was sex-linked, and this is accepted Yellow is allelomorphic with black. The heterozygous female is usually yellow-spotted or tortoiseshell, but may range in color from almost solid black to almost solid yellow. Dilute tortoiseshell is the blue-cream. Only very rarely indeed have albino cats been reported, so we may consider this outside the normal color range in cats. A fully-white coat however, combined with colored eyes does occur, and this is a simple dominant over color, and over white-spotting (patches). It is probably the incidence of white-spotting in connection with the dominant white factor which produces the blue eye.

The following is a table of those mutations in the cat which concern fancy breeding. They are set out in order of dominance:

1. Tabby, black.
2. Black (of Siamese), tabby.
3. Black, yellow (sex-linked). Heterozygotes, tortoiseshell.
4. Intense, dilute (blue, cream).
5. Full-color, silver, Burmese, Siamese (This is an albino series).
6. Coat white (eyes colored), coat colored. Dominant sub-lethal.
7. Short hair, long hair.
8. Short tail, normal tail. Homozygotes tail-less.
9. Polydactyl, normal toes.

It will be seen from the above that Siamese pattern is the nearest approach to albinism in cats. The low expression of pigmentation causes the eye to be blue. In certain light the pink eye-glow, which is characteristic of albino animals, may be seen. It will be noted also that the table shows a variation of the normal dominance, tabby, in black. Where Siamese are concerned, a dominant mutation of the extension factor has produced a black which hides the tabby pattern, though this may be revealed by a cross with recessive black individuals.

COLOR INHERITANCE IN SIAMESE

Before one can appreciate the color possibilities in Siamese, it is necessary to know something of the color make-up of the breed. We see at a glance that the pattern of the coat is different from that of other breeds. Depth of color is confined to the points, leaving the main part of the body with only the lightest of pigmentation, the shade of which varies according to the color displayed at the "points." For instance, one must expect lighter body shades in Chocolate-Pointed and Blue-Pointed than in Seal-Pointed. And the same applies to eye color, pads, and nose leathers. Whatever pigmentation there is in the coat, is more or less confined to the hair-tips. This color-pattern of the coat as a whole is familiar in rabbits and cavies, and is also present in mice, although in these it is seldom very noticeable. Each of these animals is named Himalayan—Himalayan rabbit, Himalayan cavy, Himalayan mouse. The only difference between these and the pattern on the Siamese cat is that on the Siamese the "points" color is not clean cut—it shades off into the

A Seal-Point Siamese champion before being conditioned and trimmed for showing.

If the queen is well bred and you know the faults and virtues behind her, and if you select a genetically excellent stud whose virtues compensate for your female's faults, you will never be ashamed of the kits you produce.

pale body area. The body shade darkens with age, and by reason of thermolabile pigmentation, the general pigmentation can be increased by cold.

It will be realized that all these animals—the rabbit, the cavy, the mouse, and the Siamese cat—are self-colored animals which have lost the "extension of color" factor, which is then replaced by a factor for restriction of color. In other words, the change has been brought about by mutation. How long ago the mutation occurred and precisely what course of breeding followed has never been settled definitely, but because of very early records of the coat pattern—as far back as 1793—it is obvious that the mutation occurred "in the wild," as opposed to its appearing in a cultivated stock.

A color mutation is an unexpected result from the mating of what was believed to be two normal animals of known color make-up. Now how does this unexpected result come about? I will try to explain as simply as I can in non-technical terms. As Himalayan or Siamese pattern is something between full color and albino, we will use wild "gray" as an example and explain how albino could arise as a mutation. The wild "gray" or agouti carries the pigments black, chocolate, and yellow, which are the basic colors in rabbits, cats, cavies, and mice. Now for many generations the gene would carry on normally, but all at once, for some reason or other, it ceased to function. But the next genes in the same chromosome, and which were still doing their work, carried on, and the animal seemed none the worse. In due course, the reproductive cell containing the chromosome where the affected gene used to be, took a mate, and the two proceeded to form a new animal by dividing over and over again. Also in due course, this animal made its own reproductive cells. And it made them of two kinds, the one containing a "damaged" chromosome, and the other kind, an "undamaged" one. These again in due course took partners to form new animals, and so it went on for an indefinite length of time. But note particularly this. In a state of "wild," it usually happens that a germ cell containing a "damaged" chromosome mates with one containing an "undamaged" one, and the resulting animal shows no difference in appearance, for a single "undamaged" chromosome suffices to produce all, or nearly

Misselfore Byrna, lovely Blue-Point Siamese kitten, owned by Major and Mrs. Rendall.

all, the color which the animal can produce. In other words, the gene for full color masks the effect of the "damaged" gene. Seldom in the wild, where outcrossing is the rule, though quite often in domestication where inbreeding is practiced, two germ cells, both containing "damaged" chromosomes, get together to form a new animal. This new animal is colorless, and is devoid of any gene which can produce color. So, the albino might come about as a mutation. The story of the Himalayan or Siamese coat-color-pattern mutation is just the same as the albino mutation, except that the gene in this case was not entirely "damaged." Just enough was left to allow some black, and some chocolate, (not yellow) pigment to show in the animal which ultimately resulted when two "damaged" genes got together. That is how the "Himalayan" got its pattern and chocolate-black points.

The above observations show that all Siamese cats are normal-colored cats, and carry the restriction factor. In color inheritance they behave as normal-colored cats do, but show the color in full only at their points. The factor for the body pattern is recessive to full-color, and therefore can be applied to any normal-colored cat when introduced in duplicate.

It is sometimes desired to add a fresh color-variety to an existing breed, not necessarily Siamese. The new color has to be brought in from some other established breed, and after the introduction there may be some loss of type. This ought not to condemn the new color variety, although an amount of selective breeding will be necessary to make the new color variety acceptable from the show standard point of view. In Frances Simpson's well-known book **Cats for Pleasure and Profit,** published in 1920, there are two illustrations of winning Siamese of the time. Both have heads as round as full moons. Never would they be recognized as Siamese today except for their coat pattern. This is a good example of the evolution of a type set by fanciers, and the same kind of development can be seen in most breeds when comparisons are made between old-time and present-day photographs. The evolution has taken comparatively long, but to regain a type after the introduction of some outcross is only a short-term proposition.

The three presently most popular Siamese colors are Seal-Pointed (chocolate-black), Blue-Pointed, and Chocolate-Pointed. Fanciers are advised not to cross these colors—each color should be mated only to its like. Each breeds true to its own color.

In crosses, the following would result:

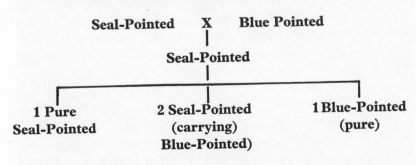

Seal-Pointed   X   Blue Pointed

Seal-Pointed

| **1 Pure Seal-Pointed** | **2 Seal-Pointed (carrying) Blue-Pointed)** | **1 Blue-Pointed (pure)** |

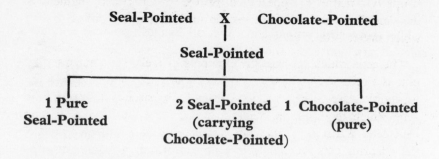

Seal-Pointed   **X**   Chocolate-Pointed

Seal-Pointed

1 Pure Seal-Pointed   **2 Seal-Pointed (carrying Chocolate-Pointed)**   **1 Chocolate-Pointed (pure)**

Fanciers are sometimes a little baffled because Seal-Pointed appears from a Chocolate-Pointed X Blue-Pointed. At first sight it looks like an unlikely result. However, it is not really so surprising when one appreciates that blue pigment and chocolate pigment are both modified forms of the same black pigment, melanin. Blue pigment is black pigment which looks blue because it has been broken up and clumped in a special way, on the microscopic scale, of course. This

Lavona Wright, well-known and respected cat judge, in the process of judging at one of the larger shows. Through the judge your efforts and knowledge as a breeder are assessed.

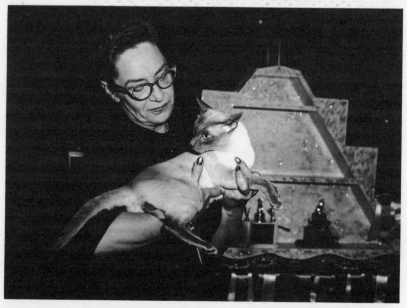

is purely a matter of appearance. Brown (or Chocolate) pigment is the same basic melanin, but broken into lumps of a different size, which makes it look brown.

The gene which controls the clumping of melanin to make it look blue is a recessive gene, that is to say, it acts only when it is present in double dose—being received from both parents. Likewise, the gene which modifies the melanin granule size, and makes it look chocolate. When you mate, say, a chocolate male to a blue female, the offspring gets the chocolate gene from the father only; but this gene has to be received from both parents if it is to make the pigment look chocolate; the offspring therefore fails to get its coat "chocolated," **i.e.;** the coat is of fundamental unmodified color, **i.e.** black. Likewise, the offspring gets the blue gene from one parent only, the mother; the gene cannot act unless it is present in double dose, so the coat is not "blued" either. The offspring, therefore, looks black.

If, on the other hand, you mate two of the offspring together, they will give blacks, blues, chocolates, and blue-chocolates (lilacs); but, of course, not in equal numbers—only one in sixteen will be lilac; three in sixteen will be blue, and three in sixteen, chocolate.

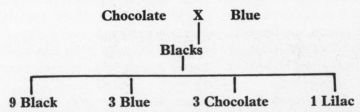

The Frost-Pointed is a new Siamese color developed in America. It has a similar relationship to blue, as chocolate has to seal. It is a blue carrying a double dilution factor. So far, I have not seen in cats a dilution of chocolate. In mice, a chocolate carrying a double dose of the pink-eye dilution is champagne silk color. Similarity of color in this instance would leave no contrast between body and points, and so the color would in Siamese be superfluous.

"Red-Points," called Siamese Red-Pointed, Red-Pointed Himalayan Shorthairs, or Flame Conchas, are a recent addition to the Siamese coat-pattern series. As mentioned, Siamese are self-colored cats with the factor for "extension of color" replaced by one for "restriction of color," the result being that full color is seen only at the points. In other words, a Seal-Pointed is a chocolate-black cat

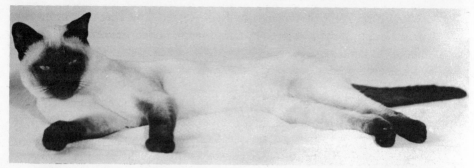

Champion Lamar's Rocco, a Chocolate male son of Ch. Lamar's Toto.
This cat was bred by Mrs. S. S. Dial and owned by Mrs. Charles Jones,
of Coronado, California.

carrying the restriction factor in duplicate; a Blue-Pointed is a blue
cat carrying the restriction factor in duplicate, and so on. Obviously,
then, to produce a Red-Pointed, one must combine the restriction
factor with the red factor, both in duplicate.

It is quite simple to breed Blue-Pointed from a Seal-Pointed
Siamese and a self-blue. Similarly, it is easy to breed Chocolate-
Pointed from a Seal-Pointed Siamese and a self-chocolate (now
available in England). But to produce Red-Pointed from Seal-
Pointed and a self-red is not quite so easy, because in cats the yellow
(red) gene is sex-linked. It follows that a red male can be bred from
a tortie or a red female irrespective of the color of his sire, while a
red female can be bred only from a mating in which both parents
have red pigment.

If the breeder decides to produce his own strain of Red-Pointed
and uses a Seal-Pointed Saimese queen and a red shorthair male,
the resulting litter will consist of tortoiseshell females and black
males. None of these kittens will show the Siamese-coat pattern,
all being Siamese-pattern hybrids; that is to say, they will carry only
one dose of the factor for Siamese coat-pattern. A tortoiseshell
female from this litter should then be mated with a Siamese male,
their predictable offspring being black, tortie, Seal-Pointed, and
Tortie-Pointed females; also black, red, Seal-Pointed, and Red-
Pointed males. With so many possible color patterns, it will require
several litters before the coveted male Red-Pointed appears. Then
further Red-Pointed males and females can be produced by mating
this Red-Pointed male back to his hybrid tortie mother or to one of
his Tortie-Pointed sisters or half sisters.

When Red-Pointed is mated to Red-Pointed, the resulting litter will contain only Red-Pointed kittens, for the Red-Pointed cat **must** be pure (or homozygous), both with respect to color genes and to the Siamese coat-pattern factor, in order to have that particular appearance.

In solid colors, sex-linked yellow mated with black gives the following results.

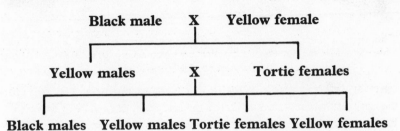

The reciprocal cross is:

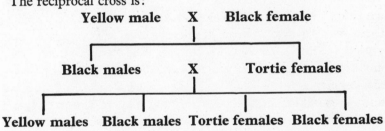

the end

INDEX.

A

Abscesses, 84, 102
Acid, 84
Adiposity, 163
Adrenals, 162
Affection, 21
Afterbirth, 69
Age, Advanced, 22
Agouti Coat Pattern, 170
Albinism, 171
Alcohol, 83
Alimentary Canal, 89
Allergy, 44, 80, 97, 132
Altenberg, 168
American-bred Cats, 30
American Cat Associations, 125
American Cat Fanciers' Association, 125
Amino Consemin, 99
Anabolics, 102
Anat: Reg.: 56, 160
Anesthesia, 83
Anesthetic, 96
Angell Memorial Hospital, 97
Antibiotics, 102
Appetite, Failing, 89
Aureomycin, 89-91
Awards, 127

B

Baby Oil, 136
Bactiracin, 102
Balhaven, 143
Bathing, 132

Bedale, 36
Beef, 44
Belly Spots, 106
Best Champion, 128, 143
Best In Show, 143
Bicarbonate of Soda, 85
Birth Canal, 68
Biscuit, 85
Biscuit, Dry Kibble, 85
Blastomeres, 152
Blood, Over-acid Conditions, 62
Blood Poisoning, 84
Blue Cat of Korat, 17
Blue Grass, 143
Blue-Pointed Siamese, 12, 118, 121,
    128, 142, 143, 172, 175, 176, 178
Body, 35, 109
Body Color, 105
Body Pattern, 175
Body Type, 52
Boric Acid Solution, 80, 84
Bread Crust, 85
Breed, New, 169
Breeder-judges, 121
Breeders, 29
Breeding, 54, 60
Breeding Capacity, 165
Breeding, Hybrid, 15
Breeding, Systematic, 168
Breeding Seasons, 61
Breeding Stock, 30
Briarry Cattery, 143
Broth, Beef, 89
Broth, Chicken, 46
Burmese Cat, 18
Buying, 29

C

Caesarean Delivery, 75

Cages, 57, 58, 137

Calcium, 44, 45, 47, 61, 65, 75, 99

Calcium Lactate, 99

Calling, 51, 52, 53, 54

Cancer, 101, 102

Carrier, 39, 56, 137

Castration, 27, 98

Cat Fanciers' Association, Inc., 125

Cat Fanciers' Federation, 125

Catarrh, 85

Cathartics, 84

Cats for Pleasure and Profit, 175

Cats Magazine, 29, 127, 129

Catteries, 57, 58, 59, 61, 143

Cavy, Himalayan, 172

Cell Division, 152

Cereal, Baby, 44

Cereal, Dry, 85

Certificate of Health, 57

Ch. Cha Wah Chirn Sa-Hai, 143

Champions, 128

Championships, 30

Championship Certificates, 30

Championship Points, 128

Championship Status, 111

Chapman, Mrs. LaVern, 143

Character, 21

Chi Charoen, 143

Chicken, 44

Ch. Chief Noda Purachatr, 142

Children, 42

Chirn Sa-Hai Cattery, 143

Chlorophyll, 61

Chocolate-Pointed Siamese, 12, 118, 120, 121, 172, 175, 176, 178

Choosing A Kitten, 31

Chromosomes, 152, 154, 155, 173

Chromosomes, Damaged, 174

Chromosomes, Sex, 157

Class, Kitten, 128

Class, Neuter, 128

Class, Novice, 128

Class, Open, 128

Claws, 101

Cleavage, 152

Clubs, 125, 128

Coat, 86, 116

Coat Pattern, 178

Coat Pattern, Agouti, 170

Coat Pattern, Striped, 170

Coat Pattern, Tabby, 170

Cobb, Mrs. Arthur, 143

Coccidiosis, 85, 86

Cod-Liver Oil, 98

Colds, 80, 91, 92

Colic, 92, 94

Collar, 25

Color, 14

Coloring, 170, 105

Color-pattern, 172

Color Pigments, 170

Color Point, 15

Color Variations, 12

Comb, Flea, 131

Combs, Mrs. Lucas, 143

Condition, 117

Constipation, 84

Contractions, 68, 70, 74

Corpora Lutea, 163

Hormone, Follicle-Stimulating, 163
Hormone, Lutealising, 163
Hormones, 102, 162
Horner, Mrs. N., 143
Horsemeat, 46
Ch. H.R.H. of Ebon Mask, 47, 110
Hospital, Veterinary, 90

J

Jealousy, 25
Jennings, H. S., 168
J. Gen.: Physiol.: 13, 129
J. of Hed:, 168
Judges, 122
Judging, 105, 121

I

Illness, at Shows, 127
Importations, 29
Inbreeding, 116, 164
Infantilism, 163
Infertility, 163
Inflammatory Exudates, 102
Infections, 81, 82, 83, 85, 86, 88, 89, 90, 91, 92, 96, 97
Infections, Ears, 82, 83
Infections, Fungus, 96
Infections, Intestinal Tract, 85
Infections, Virus, 91
Infectious Enteritis, 30, 32, 88, 89, 90, 102
Inheritance, 111
Inheritance, Color, 172
Inherited Characteristics, 152, 157
Inoculations, 30
Inoculations, Enteritis, 90
Insemination, Artificial, 167
International Units (I.U.), 163
Intestinal Tract, 89
Iodine, 97
Islets of Langerhans, 162

K

Kidney Gravel, 99
Kidneys, 90
Kinked Tail, 12, 36, 111, 113
Kohlus, Mrs. Julia, 143
Kwan Yin, 143

L

Labor, 67, 68, 72, 158
Lactation, 160
Lamb, 46
Lancing, 84
Lavender Cat, 121
Lead, 25
Legs, 35
Litter, 72
Liver, 90
Liver Upset, 44
Long-Haired Siamese, 15
Luteal Scars, 164

M

MacDowell, 160
Maiden Queens, 60
Malayan Persian, 15
Malformation, 111
Mammals, 158, 167
Mammary Glands, 159
Mating, 60, 62, 113
Matings, Brother-to-Sister, 168
Meat, 44, 45, 61, 85
Meat, Rabbit, 44
Melanin Pigment, 171, 176
Mendelian Scheme, 149
Metastasis, 101, 102
Milk, 47, 159
Milk, Acid, 85
Milk, Evaporated, 47, 48
Milk, Skim, 44
Milk, Whole, 44, 61
Milk of Bismuth, 85
Milk of Magnesia, 84, 85, 92, 95
Milk Production, 163
Millbrook, 143
Mineral Oil, 84, 99
Mouse, Black-eyed white, 167
Mouse, Himalayan, 172
Mutation, Color, 173
Mutation, Dominant, 172
Mutations, 149, 171

N

Nails, 101
Neck, 111

Gr. Ch. Nee Yang, 143
Neomycin, 102
Nervousness, 133
Neutering, 26, 98
Newton, 143
Norton, Mrs. Karl, 142
Nourishment, 149
Nursing, 45
Nutrition, 149, 167

O

Obstructions, 95, 96
O'Donovan, Mrs. Beth, 143
Onychectomy, 99
Organizations, 125
Oriental Cattery, 143
Ch. Oriental Nanki Poo, 143
Outcrossing, 169
Ovarian Rhythm, 164
Ovaries, 162, 163
Overfeeding, 76, 94
Overweight, 118
Ovum, 152, 167
Oxidation, 171

P

Panda, 17
Panleucopenia, 88
Parathyroid, 162
Parturition, 167
Pathologists, 147
Pedigree, 29, 30, 51, 52
Pedigree Forms, 170
Pedigree, Multiple, 150

S

Sacred Siamese, 11

Saline Solution, 80, 89

Salve, Bear Grease, 135

Sanitary Pan, 39, 40

Sapphire Blue, 36, 115

Scratching, 101

Scrotum, 165

Seal-Pointed Siamese, 12, 118, 120,
121, 128, 172, 175, 176, 177, 178

Secondary Sex Characteristics, 164

Secretions, 162, 164

Sex Chromosomes, 157

Sex-linked, 171

Sexual Development, 163

Sexual Underdevelopment, 163

Shampoo, 132

Shawnee, 143

Shedding, 99

Shetland Ponies, 167

Shipment, Air, 57

Shipping, 56

Shipping Expenses, 56

Shire Horses, 167

Show, All-breed, 126, 128

Show Entries, 143

Show Proceeds, 129

Show Rules, 125, 126

Show, Short-Hair, 127

Show Winners, 142, 143

Shows, 15, 30, 101, 105, 122, 126,
127, 128, 134

Siam Cattery, 142

Siama, 143

Siamese Legends, 12

Siamese Section of the American Cat
Fanciers' Association, 118

Siamese Specialty Clubs, 127

Sickness, 131

Silken Cattery, 143

Simpson, Frances, 175

Size, 109

Skin Disorders, 96, 98

Skin Eruptions, 97

Skin Sack, 68, 70, 158

Sodium Caprylate, 97

Sodium Pentothal, 96

Southwood Cattery, 143

Spaying, 27, 98

Specialties, 127, 128

Specialty Club, 127

Sperm, 151, 154

Spermatozoon, 164, 167

Spotlight Cattery, 143

Spray, 27, 61

Stackhouse, Mr.-Mrs. Howard, 143

Standard, 105

Starches, 75

Sterility, 160, 164, 165

Stomach, Upset, 94

Strep Throat, 89

Streptomycin, 90, 102

Stud, 51, 52, 54, 56, 59, 60, 61, 111

Stud Book, 19, 30

Stud Fees, 55, 56

Stud House, 57, 59, 61

Stud Quarters, 57

Stud Rooms, 59

Sukianga Cattery, 143

Sulfa Drugs, 85, 91

Sulfaguanadine, 85

Sulfasuxidine, 85
Sulfathiazole, 85
Sulfathiazole Ointment, 80

T

Tail, 35, 36, 111, 113
Tail, Bobbed, 111
Tail, Double-Kinked, 111
Tail, Hooked, 111
Tail, Kink, 12, 36, 111, 113
Tail-lessness, 167
Tang Wong Cattery, 58
Tapeworm, 86, 87, 88
Tartar, 47
Teat, 159
Teeth, 47
Telegony, 165
Temperature, 58
Terramycin, 91, 102
Testes, 162
Tetracycline, 102
Thymus, 163
Thyroid, 162, 163
Ticking, 135
Tortoiseshell Cat, 157, 171
Travel, 27, 137

U

Ultraviolet Lamps, 61, 92
Umbilical Cord, 70, 71
Umbilical Hernia, 70
Umbilicus, 158

Under-feeding, 165
United Cat Federation, 125
Urinary Infections, 102
Urotropine, 99
Uterine Cysts, 51
Uterus, 158

V

Vaccine, Feline Anti-distemper, 90
Vaccine, Homologous
Variations, 149, 150
Variations, Individual, 149
Vegetables, 46
Vertebrae, 111
Veterinarian, 79, 84, 85, 86, 96, 98,
    101, 127
Veterinary Hospitals, 90
Viosterol, 79
Virus Infection, 91
Vitamin A, 45, 46, 61, 79, 99
Vitamin B, 47, 99
Vitamin D, 45, 79, 80, 98
Vitamins, 45, 46, 47, 61, 75, 79,
    80, 98, 99
Voice, 18, 26, 27, 53
Gr. Ch. Vee Rois Lantara Gene, 143

W

Wade, Mrs., 36
Ch. Wan Tutswan, 142
Water, 76
Whims About Food, 23